THE GREATEST WONDER OF ALL

Sermons for Lent and Easter
Cycle C Gospel Texts

BY JOHN M. BRAATEN

C.S.S Publishing Co., Inc.
Lima, Ohio

THE GREATEST WONDER OF ALL

Copyright © 1991 by
The C.S.S. Publishing Company, Inc.
Lima, Ohio

All rights reserved. No part of this publication may be reproduced, stored in a retrieval system, or transmitted in any form or by any means, electronic, mechanical, photocopying, recording, or otherwise, without the prior permission of the publisher. Inquiries should be addressed to: The C.S.S. Publishing Company, Inc., 628 South Main Street, Lima, Ohio 45804.

Library of Congress Cataloging-in-Publication Data
Braaten, John M., 1938-
  The greatest wonder of all : sermons for Lent and Easter cycle C gospel texts / by John M. Braaten.
    p.   cm.
  ISBN 1-55673-313-5
    1. Lenten sermons.   2. Eastertide—Sermns.   3. Sermons, American.
  I. Title.
  BV4277.B72   1991
  252'.62—dc20
                                                                91-7424
                                                                   CIP

9134 / ISBN 1-55673-313-5   PRINTED IN U.S.A.

Dedicated
in honor of my mother, Elmyra Braaten,
and
in memory of my father, Pastor M. A. Braaten,
who kept feeding me faith when I was preoccupied
with fun until at last I found my joy in Jesus Christ.

Table Of Contents

Foreword — 7

Preface — 9

Ash Wednesday — 11
    The Pitfalls Of Practicing Piety
    Matthew 6:1-6, 16-21

Lent 1 — 19
    Our Christian I.D.
    Luke 4:1-13

Lent 2 — 27
    Finding Our Roots
    Luke 9:28-36 [RC]
    Luke 13:31-35 [C, L]

Lent 3 — 35
    Planted For A Purpose
    Luke 13:1-13

Lent 4 — 41
    The Story Of The Scandalized Neighbors
    Luke 15:11-24

Lent 5 — 49
    Two "R-Rated" Stories
    John 8:1-11 [RC]
    John 12:1-8 [C]
    Luke 20:9-14 [L]

Passion/Palm Sunday — 59
    That's Our God For You
    Luke 19:28-40

Maundy Thursday — 65
    Portrait Of A Powerful Servant
    Luke 22:7-20 [C, L]
    John 13:1-15 [RC]

Good Friday   71
    The King Who Came To Die
    John 19:16b-22

Easter   77
    Good News From A Graveyard
    John 20:1-18

Easter 2   83
    A Word For All Reasons
    John 20:19-31

Easter 3   89
    Act III; Scene 2
    John 21:1-14

Easter 4   95
    Safe With The Shepherd
    John 10:22-30

Easter 5   103
    A Strange Kind Of Glory
    John 13:31-35

Easter 6   109
    A Farewell Gift
    John 14:23-29

Easter 7   117
    Beyond Togetherness
    John 17:20-26

The Day of Pentecost   123
    The Greatest Wonder Of All!
    John 14:8-17, 25-27 [C]
    John 15:26-27; 16:4b-11 [L]
    John 20:19-23 [RC]

C — Common Lectionary
L — Lutheran Lectionary
RC — Roman Catholic Lectionary

Foreword

Some sermons read well, and these do, but having heard many of these sermons preached during a very difficult time in my own life, I know that they speak to the real needs of the congregation. John is above all else a pastor who feels the pulse of his congregation — a mature pastor who loves to preach. These sermons reflect it.

He has a style of preaching that pulls you right into the sermon and carries you along with it. Carefully thought out and structured, they are filled with little gems that delight: "A funny thing happened to God on his way to earth. Nobody recognized him," or "The silence screamed in their ears as Jesus washed their feet."

Every sermon has an intriguing insight, a bit of a twist to the text. That was my problem as I read these sermons. I often stopped to think (sometimes to agree, sometimes to disagree). But then, isn't that the value of a book of sermons for a preacher?

You will be blessed as you read but if you are a preacher you will also be stimulated — not to copy or imitate, but to "go out and do likewise," to preach to your people the good news about Jesus Christ in a personal and interesting manner. These sermons will trigger your imagination and make you eager to apply their insights in your own unique way.

Pastor Robert Onkka
Bethel Lutheran Church — 1990

Preface

On the wall, facing my desk, hangs a plaque given to me when I became the administrative pastor of Bethel Lutheran Church. The words, though Paul's, mirror my own feelings: "I thank Christ Jesus, our Lord, who has given me strength and who judged me faithful enough to call me into his service (1 Timothy 1:12)."

And as if that were not enough, I have been given the privilege by God and by my congregation to proclaim the gospel! What a gracious gift, to be given license to proclaim good news to people who have been inundated by bad news all week long. They come faithfully with eager ears and heartfelt longing to hear a message of hope and strength from the Lord. The look of yearning in the people's eyes fuels this pastor's heart with hope and whets his appetite for preaching week after week.

I am glad it is good news that our Lord asks us to bear into the world. I remember hearing that in ancient Rome messengers were the postal service of the day. A man was given a sealed message and a destination. When he arrived at his appointed place the seal was broken and the message read. If the news were good he was invited to a celebration. When the news was dire, there was a good chance he would be killed! Gratefully, God has given us good news to announce!

Preaching is the love of my ministerial life, even though the awkward words which I utter from the pulpit bear only the slightest resemblance to the magnificent, inspired thoughts which flash all too briefly through my mind. Unfortunately those visions are difficult to incarnate in coherent ences. Fortunately my beloved people are receptive, an ly Spirit mighty, so the congregation gets fed anyway — praise God!

I have attempted in my sermons to use inclusive language. All preachers need to be sensitive to that. In reference to God I have tried to avoid the male pronoun. I have employed it only in those situations when, to continue to repeat the noun

"God," would have been awkward or would have sounded like stuttering, both of which draw the hearer away from the message and into the language; that is counter-productive. As an English student, it is my hope that perceptive and respected linguists will soon come up with a pronoun which refers only to the Deity and thus resolve the whole matter.

I am deeply indebted to a number of people who have made this book possible. I especially thank my wife, Julie, and my daughter, Heather, who sacrificed their time with me that this publication could become a reality. Their love and support create a backdrop against which I am able to see the glorious overtones of the gospel so that I am able to preach the good news with confidence.

The profound impact that Pastor Richard Holleque has had on my preaching cannot be overstated. The seminal thoughts of many of my sermons were taken from notes I had scribbled on bulletins while Dick preached.

A special word of thanks to Myrna Lyng, of Mayville, N.D., who pored over my sermons in an attempt to make me sound more fluent than I am. I deeply appreciate her not only because of the countless hours she put in as editor of this project, but for her subtle humor, her friendship and her honesty.

I am grateful to C.S.S. Publishing House for the invitation to participate in this lectionary preaching series; it has been humbling and challenging, and I have grown in appreciation for those who must not have full-time jobs and are therefore able to write many books!

Finally, I thank the members of Bethel Lutheran Church who week after week come to me in winsome ways saying, "The gospel is important to me, thank you for your message." It convinces me that preaching remains a preeminent force in spreading the word of God. I am also persuaded that preaching, like all other works done for the sake of the Lord, is not in vain. That's a wonderful promise to preach in!

John M. Braaten
Rochester, Minnesota
August 30, 1990

Ash Wednesday
Matthew 6:1-6, 16-21

The Pitfalls Of Practicing Piety

I have never liked the word "beware." It always seems to be written in intimidating block letters which suggest life-threatening consequences. The word brings to mind an experience I had as a 12-year-old paperboy. Entering a customer's yard I encountered a collie which, without provocation, charged me with fangs bared, knocking off my glasses and hurling me to the ground. I still remember its moist, rancid breath in my face. Hearing my screams, neighbors came and rescued me. That event not only changed my attitude toward dogs, it changed my life, forever.

That experience surfaced one day when I was on my way to visit prospective members, a delightful couple whom I had met earlier in church. As I approached their yard, the sign "Beware Of Dog" sped adrenalin through my system and nearly drove me away. Then I heard barking. The dog rounding the corner was not a collie but a much smaller dog, a cocker spaniel; still, I froze. I am sure it sensed my terror and was enjoying mastery of the situation. Unable to move, I had to wait until the owner came to rescue me by inviting me into their house. I mentioned that I thought it strange that their dog should be loose when the sign gave a warning.

"Oh, that," the man said, "the sign is meant to fool salesmen and prowlers; everyone in the neighborhood knows that Suzie wouldn't hurt anyone."

Jesus isn't trying to fool anyone. He places the "beware" in our text today for the precise reason that we can easily wander into danger in our spiritual life and put our souls in peril. That word of warning is especially timely as we worship this evening. Traditionally, Ash Wednesday has been a day of repentance; that is a good and godly act, but it is precisely at that point that Jesus comes to us and says, "Beware of practicing your piety before others." Practicing piety is the effort we make to impress everyone with our goodness, or our rightness, or our moral superiority.

The world in which Jesus lived was rampant with examples. The Jewish *Talmud* describes several. For instance there were the "Shoulder Pharisees" who carefully obeyed the laws but wore their good deeds on their shoulders, as it were, trying to publicize how virtuous they were and how many wonderful acts they had done. They obeyed the Law, but did so in order to be seen by others.

There were also "Bleeding Pharisees." In the Palestine of Jesus' day women were held in low esteem, and men of religion were not to talk to a woman in public. But these fellows went even further. They would not even look at a woman in public. They would shut their eyes as they walked, and as a result, bumped into walls, trees, or whatever was in their path. Therefore they bruised and wounded themselves and those bleeding sores gained them the reputation of being especially pious.

"Tumbling Pharisees" are a third type mentioned in the *Talmud*. These men walked with exaggerated humility. They demonstrated this by refusing to lift their feet off the ground and so they tripped over anything in their path. Their posturing was intended to advertise their piety so that in reality it was motivated by pride.

Strange as those Pharisees appear, they have no corner on hypocrisy. You and I are not unlike those religious leaders; we find ways to parade our piety before others in many different ways.

Take the example William Styron draws for us in his book, *Lie Down in Darkness*. Helen Loftis, divorced from her alcoholic husband and alienated from her rebellious daughter, decides to pull her family together for the daughter's marriage. She will impress everyone, she decides, by presenting only the face of humility and courage and gentle good will. She carefully connives to make herself look good. Of course she is being dishonest, but "Oh, what was honesty, anyway? She could discard honest intentions to make this day come true. "Anything, anything," she had said to herself . . . "anything at all." Anything that people should know Helen Loftis was a good mother, a successful mother. Anything that people should know: it was Helen Loftis, that suffering woman, who had brought together the broken family."[1]

Consider all the gossip which travels like wildfire among us; all of it, all of it poorly veiled attempts to place ourselves above others. Put-downs, criticisms, pot-shots: all are ways we practice our piety, trying to elevate ourselves by judging others. There's a certain amount of twisted pleasure to be experienced when piously practicing character assassination. It happens all the time.

Do not imagine that pastors are immune from well-rehearsed religiosity. There is no greater temptation in the ministry than to be a good pastor so that people will point and say, "That's our pastor. We really like him or her." Do you think that could be anything but music to our ears? Why do we become pastors? Submission to God's will? Complete reliance upon Christ? A desire to give our lives away like a suffering servant? We trust that those things are part of a pastor's call into the ministry, but we are like you; we want to be loved and accepted and therefore must confess that our good deeds can be motivated more by a desire to be liked by our parishioners than out of love for them or the Lord. However, this practice of piety isn't reserved only for the clergy.

When any one of us examines ourselves carefully, we are sure to find that we are secretly living with the thought pattern of reward and punishment. That is, deep down, the motivation for our kindly, unselfish acts is governed by our desire for prestige, or honor, or a good reputation before God and one another. Helmut Thielicke, the great German preacher asks, "Do we not all strut a bit upon a lighted stage and assume poses, because the good Lord and our neighbors and friends are sitting in the audience and we would like to have some applause and lots of flowers and handshakes?"[2] Clearly our need for the warm glow of approval is often disguised as altruism.

That's why Jesus puts his "beware" in front of this statement, ". . . in order to be seen by men; for then you will have no reward from your Father who is in heaven." You will be seen by others, that's all. When people give in order to be seen by others they get recognized; they find their name on the list of donors. They get their reward then they get credit for what they have done. But it's a pretty hollow satisfaction compared to that which comes to those who give, not because they will get good press, but because they are in love with the cause; they believe in it. So they are moved to invest, not only their gifts, but also their lives.

Jesus says there are real rewards in life, although Christians who focus on grace as God's undeserved gift, tend to be a little embarrassed about such talk. But Jesus was quite clear on the matter. He said there is such a thing as rewards, or consequences. Not rewards in the sense that one earns them. But outcomes. Results which follow every choice we take, every decision we make, every road we embark on.

Some seem to feel that rewards have no place in religious life; virtue ought to be its own reward. A person ought to be good and do good simply and only for goodness sake; it's called "the theology of the empty cup." That theology emphasizes complete self-sacrificing service, reflected pretty well in the following words of the good Christian hymn: "Nothing in my hand I bring; Simply to thy cross I cling; Naked come to thee for dress; Helpless, look to thee for grace; Foul, I to the fountain fly; Wash me, Savior, or I die."

It's true, and it's great. But Jesus still talks about rewards, consequences. The Psalmist cried out, "The Lord is my Shepherd, I shall not want." Later he said, "My cup runs over." But we are to notice very carefully the nature of the reward. What kind of rewards are they? What kinds of outcomes can you expect if you live obediently and faithfully? Well, it doesn't have much to do with having a higher standard of living. That isn't the promise. It doesn't necessarily mean a long life, or a healthier one. It doesn't even promise a happier one; Paul discovered that.

What are the rewards like? Listen to what our Lord says, "You have been faithful in little things," and you will be rewarded, how? "I will set you over much (Matthew 25:21)." In other words he said, "Because you have been faithful in a few things, I will give you greater responsibility!"

Do you understand? The reward for being faithful is a life requiring greater faithfulness. The reward for being responsible in this world in small ways is to be given responsibility in larger ways. The reward for doing hard work is the opportunity for doing harder work. The reward for loving is the capacity to love more, to understand more, to forgive more, to become involved more deeply. Is that the kind of reward we are looking for?

I have read that more and more people in industry and in the military are refusing to rise from the ranks when they are offered a promotion. They turn it down. Why? Because a promotion means heavier responsibilities; it means making more decisions, it means taking more work home at night, it means increased anxiety. This is the reward that God holds out to us. To some it sounds more like punishment. Only those who love God and desire above all else to serve him will ever understand.

Robert Caulk, a German pioneer in bacteriology, struggled for years working in a shed, working with apparatus tied together with strings. Then one day some of his friends called him to the attention of the German government and he was given an important position in the health office in Berlin. There he was given a fine laboratory with all kinds of modern equipment and a couple of assistants. He was given a generous grant of money and Robert Caulk was overjoyed. Why? Simply because now he could do more, because now he could expend himself to the tune of 60 to 70 hours a week doing the kinds of things he knew had to be done with his guinea pigs and his test tubes. He now had his reward, the opportunity to work harder, to give more of himself, to serve.

That kind of a reward doesn't have much to do with knowing for sure you are one of God's favorites. You can't reduce it to self-centered consumerism where the one with the most is best blessed by God. There are rewards in the Christian life and they are abundant, but they seem strange to the person who does not possess a vibrant faith, absolutely unintelligible to anyone who does not love God. Nor does the great song, the great verse of hymnody make any rhyme or reason at all, "Nothing in my hand I bring; Simply to thy cross I cling. Naked come to thee for dress; Helpless, look to thee for grace; Foul, I to the mountain fly; Wash me, Savior, or I die."

Not that piety is bad. It is the practice of piety, its rote rehearsal which is so distasteful to Jesus. Those who practice piety do good for the recognition it gives them. True piety, on the other hand, seeks to honor God for the wonder of creation and the greater wonder of Jesus Christ. The practice of piety centers on the deed, while true piety seeks to serve a need. Mock piety makes me feel good; genuine piety enables someone else to rejoice. False piety glorifies me; true piety glorifies Christ.

So we are given the privilege of piety, to do good so that others may see what we do and give glory to God. That kind of life-giving, Jesus says, will be rewarded. He once put it this way, "They that have given up brothers, sisters, father and mother, or children for my sake will receive a hundred fold (Matthew 19:29)." Imagine in this life having hundreds of mothers, hundreds of fathers, hundreds of brothers and sisters, hundreds of children to love and care for, to agonize over; to weep with and to rejoice with. That is the reward, the glory and the wonder of Christians who give generously, pray sincerely, live life compassionately and lay up for themselves treasures in heaven. Amen.

Heavenly Father, we confess our sins to you but then rely on our meager acts of goodness for our salvation. In your great mercy transform our hearts and minds that we may accept your gift of salvation and rest only on the merits of the resurrection of Jesus Christ. During this Lenten season send your Spirit to constantly remind us of who we are that, for the joy that is set before us, we simply and faithfully offer ourselves to your service. In Jesus' precious name. Amen.

---

1. Styron, William. *Lie Down in Darkness.* A Signet Book. The Bobbs-Merrill Company, Inc. 1951. p. 261.

2. Thielicke, Helmut. *Life Can Begin Again.* Fortress Press. Philadelphia, 1963. pp. 82-83.

Lent 1
Luke 4:1-13

Our Christian I.D.

Given that you and I are reasonably good people, it probably does not amaze you to read that Jesus was able to overcome temptation. After all, like me, you've probably been able to do it yourself, many times. Admittedly, we have also caved in to temptation innumerable times, but for a person with Jesus' devotion and strength, eluding the tempter's entrapment must have been a piece of cake.

That assumption is based on that belief that temptation is merely the urge to do something wrong. It is the desire to do something which will benefit one's self but which, if done, would violate the laws of God or society.

For instance, you walk through a store and you see something you would like to own, but you don't have the cash, so into your mind pops the thought of stealing it. Or, you have been given the responsibility of collecting money for a project and since no one really knows what you have gathered, and you are a little short of cash, you think about embezzling some of it. Or you are in a tight situation and the easiest way to weasel out of it, you think, would be to lie. We come across events like these in our lives and we call them temptations.'' I guess they are that, but they really don't convey the depth of what the Bible has in mind when it speaks of temptations.

The temptations of Jesus in our text were not designed so much to get Jesus to do something wrong, as they were attempts to get Jesus to lose sight of who he was, and leave unfulfilled the mission God had given him. So what is involved in Jesus' wilderness experience with Satan is something far deeper than merely disobeying the commandments, and far more dangerous. There was something very frightening in what went on; we need to look at it carefully.

The gospel story this morning follows on the heels of Jesus' baptism. When he was baptized in the Jordan River, you remember, he heard the voice of the Heavenly Father saying, "You are my beloved Son." Now, out in the barren wilderness, on the other side of the Jordan, he hears Satan saying, "If you are the Son of God . . ." If you are the Son of God. The devil is suggesting that there is some doubt about who he is. In effect, he asks, "How can you, Jesus of Nazareth, a poor Galilean carpenter, be the long-awaited Messiah? How can you lead without followers? How can you, with only a minimal education, consider becoming a great leader of Israel? Who will ever believe you, Jesus?"

Don't you see how subtle Satan is, not in persuading Jesus to do something wrong, but in getting Jesus to question who he is?

What is at stake here is the matter of identity. Who was Jesus? And our identity; who are we? The most important thing about you is the matter of who you are, your I.D., your identity.

One of the saddest conditions a person can face in life is amnesia, when one doesn't know who they are. It is frightening when one does not understand what life is about, when one can see no purpose in life. That which made Willy Lohman such a pathetic character in Arthur Miller's play, *Death of a Salesman,* is revealed by his son Biff after Willie committed suicide; he says that at the heart of his father's problems was that he didn't know who he was.

Knowing your identity, who you are and whose you are, is essential to your wholeness as God's child and to your awareness of what God wants you to do with your life. So Satan's primary objective is not getting you to do something wrong, something bad, but to cause you to lose track of who you are — to lose your identity — to lose your sense of belonging to the family of God.

The ways Satan tries to convince us that we do not deserve to be God's beloved are most often subtle, clever and deadly. And these temptations, like the temptations of Christ, are far more insidious than any impulse to disobey the commandments.

Consider this tricky question, "If you are a child of God, then why don't you feel more like one?" It's deadly because sometimes we don't feel much like a beloved member of God's family. The implication is that if you don't feel like one, then maybe you're not one. Maybe you are not a child of God, maybe you are not a Christian.

Or how about this terrible temptation, "If you are a child of God, then why don't you act like one?" I know there are times when I don't act like one. How about you? Why do I have the thoughts I sometimes have? Why do I do the things I sometimes do? And why don't I seem to be getting much better? Me a Christian? I sometimes wonder. How can I be a Christian if I don't live as a Christian should live? Satan is filled with glee when we begin to ask that question of ourselves: Am I a Christian?

Even sneakier is the question: "Are you sure you're a real Christian?" As though there are Christians, and then there are the real Christians. Now we have moved from self-examination to comparing ourselves to one another and if we don't watch it we will find ourselves trying to usurp Christ's role as judge, determining who is saved and who is not.

A woman came into a pastor's office some years ago. She told the pastor she had been attending worship at one of the local churches, but as far as she could see there were only two real Christians in the whole congregation, and the pastor wasn't one of them!

Well, where did we ever get the idea we could rate our Christian identity? Maybe it's because we have a picture in our minds of what a real Christian is, and then we compare others to that "ideal." Or we compare ourselves, and it causes us to doubt and ask, "Am I a real Christian?"

The word "wilderness" in our text was often used by the Jewish people as a symbol for being lost — to be spiritually lost. Sometimes we don't feel like children of God. Sometimes we sure don't act like it. So it seems as though we are in a wilderness, not knowing who we are, not knowing where we are, experiencing the fear of being lost, of being cut adrift in life.

What do we do then? Well, what did Jesus do out in the wilderness of his temptation? He went back to the Scriptures that he learned as a child. He went back to the stories which had been told to him at home and in the synagogue. He remembered the things God had done for him; he recalled the truths God had spoken to him and the people of Israel.

Our Old Testament lesson this morning underlines how the Hebrew people in those days understood who they were. They continually reminded themselves that God had chosen them. They had not elected God; God had sought them out, selected them. It began with Abraham, a wandering Armenian, 2000 years before Christ. God promised that Abraham and his descendants would become a great nation, and that all the rest of the world would be blessed through them. Later God delivered that people out of slavery and brought them to the land he had promised to them. And all along he sent prophets to them with achingly beautiful claims, "Fear not, O Israel, for I have redeemed you, I have called you by name, you are mine (Isaiah 43:1)." But those rebellious people turned from God, so he let their sins catch up with them, and they were exiled from their homeland. When they repented, however, God brought them back again, and they came back with tears streaming down their faces because they knew that God's promises to them had not been broken. Though they had been faithless, God had remained faithful.

What does this history lesson have to do with us? Just about everything. For our identity as children of God rests on the fact that God's claim has been laid upon us. Jesus said, "You did not choose me, but I chose you and appointed you that you should go and bear fruit . . . (John 15:16)." Nowhere is it written that our acceptance by Jesus is dependent upon how we feel or upon anything we've done or not done. Our life as Christians doesn't rest upon feelings, or upon how certain we are that we are Christians. None of that counts, for Christ has claimed us. Beginning with baptism he claimed us, which is something he did, not something we did. And Christ has been claiming us as his own and offering to fulfill the promises of Scripture ever since.

The New Testament lesson for this Sunday reminds us that God's message of grace is always near us, as near as our own hearts. It says that God accepts everyone who comes to him. In Paul's words, "Everyone who calls on the Lord for help will be saved." Everyone? Everyone! Everyone is invited to come, with the promise that whoever does come will be received, accepted, forgiven, loved.

Do you believe that? Do you want it? Do you want Jesus as your Lord and Savior? Then you are a Christian! You may not always be a very faithful one. You may not always be a very strong one. You may not always feel like one. You may not always act like one, but you are a child of God because Christ has chosen you, and enabled you to acknowledge his claim on your life. Some of you, if you're anything like me, need to be encouraged every day to step out into the joy and freedom of believing that that's the way it is, so you can stop wondering who you are and what you are, and can press on as God's beloved children in this world.

In some churches when babies are baptized they are given a candle; it is to be lit each year on the anniversary of their baptism. Those candles are given as a visual reminder to them, and to others in the family, that he or she is a child of God. It's a sign of assurance of who we are — or better, whose we are. Maybe there isn't anything more important that we can do for our children than to keep reminding them of who they are, and whose they are. They belong to Jesus. He chose them. And he chose you. And glory of glories, he chose me. Me! Christ claims that you and I are worthy of being one of his dearly beloved — worth dying for, and worth returning for, in order that we might be his . . . forever.

When Martin Luther became depressed, he saw it as a temptation of Satan and he would turn to his ancient foe and cry out, "I am baptized. I am baptized." He needed the assurance of his identity, that he belonged to Jesus. If he were going to carry out the great work God had given him to do he needed to be sure that even though his faith might waver, God's all-encompassing love would not. He needed the assurance that he was held, held firmly in that mighty grip of mercy.

Out there in the wilderness Jesus was tempted and tested as Satan tried to get him to compromise his high calling. "Turn the stones into bread!" Not just for himself, but for the world. Jesus knew how poor they were, how hungry they were. But we humans cannot live by bread alone. Providing bread for the starving was important, but that is not why he had come; he would not substitute the good for the best.

Or how about the temptation to fall down and worship Satan? Why not? Satan implies, "Think of yourself Jesus. Why suffer the rejection of people? Show them that you have the right stuff to be the Messiah. Show them that you are a winner; they will get on the bandwagon and follow you up to the very jaws of hell. Why go through the agony of betrayal, denial and desertion by your closest friends? Why endure the suffering of the cross? Think Jesus, you have to look out for yourself. You deserve to be happy; you ought to enjoy life and it will cost you so little, just bow down before me. Everyone will understand, even the Father; it just makes good sense. Don't be so hard on yourself."

But Jesus had come with a mission that was far more important than merely trying to get the most out of life, and far greater than helping others to become successful. He had come to illustrate God's love in a unique and sacrificial way. He had come to give his all, to usher in a whole new age of mercy, forgiveness and eternal life. He would not substitute the good for the best. He would not exchange the high for the highest.

So in the midst of the temptations which seek to lure us into forgetting who we are and what we are to be about in this world, comes the insistent invitation from God to the highest and best of all callings. A Christian calling which says that we are to live out the gospel in our everyday lives. We are to be visible expressions of the loving, caring God who has come to us in Jesus Christ. Every day we are tempted to abandon our calling, to sink into what is ultimately a deadly way of life, living merely as consumers in God's world, taking the easy way out, living primarily for ourselves. Living for, what one man called, the big seven: Money, fame, success, power, health, security, and pleasure.

It is doubtful that the everyday sins which plague us and supply tinder for the fires of our guilt will cause us to lose out on salvation, especially if we come to God daily in repentance and rely on our Savior's forgiveness. Nor are the big trials of life, the great crises, our greatest danger, because chances are, they will draw us back to the Heavenly Father for the security of his power and grace. Not even our doubts and rebellion offer the greatest peril, for we usually discover, as a friend read in devotions recently, ". . . that God knows all about it and follows us into our darkness; and there, where we thought finally to escape him, we run straight into his arms." No, our greatest threat is a way of life which day in and day out, crowds out faith, elbows God out, takes over in subtle ways, forming and shaping us in such a way that we forget who we are and what God has called us to do in this world.

So what are we to do? Well, out there in the wilderness our Lord nothing to rely on except the old, familiar, words of Scripture, "One does not live by bread alone." "Do not put the Lord your God to the test." "Worship the Lord your God and serve him only!" There's a good chance that Jesus didn't feel much like the Son of God out there in the wastelands, because he was tired, hungry and exhausted. But he had the Scriptures. He knew that God was within him, and he gave himself to obeying what he knew and believed about God.

The same is true for us. Often in the midst of temptation, the only thing which enables us to do battle with Satan is our faith in Christ and his clear promises. But there is tremendous power in that. Someone has said, "Sometimes indeed, God seems to take everything from us . . . but never himself." Never himself!

Our Lord's question is simply this: "Am I not enough for you, O you of little faith?" He will never take himself from you. I cannot imagine anything more strengthening, more encouraging as you face the temptations and testings of this life. God will be present for you now and forever.

I invite you to cling to Jesus and say your prayers. Say them with others, and say them alone, asking:

O Lord God, where I have drifted into a compromise with the world, loving its gods, admiring its ways, wanting its rewards, take us into the solitude of some wilderness of your making, and there let us speak our "yes" to you for the glory of your name and for the salvation of our souls. For Jesus' sake. Amen.

Lent 2
Luke 9:28-36 [RC]
Luke 13:31-35 [C, L]

Finding Our Roots

Ever since Alex Haley's novel, *Roots*, hit the bookstands in the mid-70s, there has been an increasing number of people interested in their heritage. I know one man who bought a computer primarily to keep track of his family tree. He has also taken a liking to trans-Atlantic flying because it enables him to get back to his roots by searching for his forebears in their own country.

Parish secretaries are often called upon to do research for people investigating their family heritage. It is clear that many persons have been motivated to search through history in an attempt to find their roots. As one newspaper columnist wrote, "The once fabled rootless Americans are realizing that the people who formed the foundations of their heritage are important. And more than that, they are enjoying their quest, for there is satisfaction and security in finding one's roots."

Finding our roots, unveiling the people of our past, is a process that helps us discover who we are by looking at where we came from. But it's only the beginning. Even more telling is the question of where we have set our roots for daily life. What motivates our day-to-day existence? Or I could put the question to you in this way, "What's the biggest thing in your life?" What's most important to you?

Some might answer, "My home and family, everything revolves around them." Or someone else, "My country, first, last and always." Some might even say, "My work, my work means everything to me; without that, I'd be lost." Others might answer, "My youth. The important thing in my life right now is the fact that I'm young." Many would simply reply, "Health and happiness." Don't we say, "If you've got your health, you've got just about everything?" And we all want to be happy.

These are certainly important facts of life, the foliage which enhances our daily living. Then we must ask, "What if these things go?" What happens when your home, your family is crushed by news of a fatal illness or shattered by the death of a loved one? What if you lose your job? Or if your income no longer pays the bills? What if you wake up one day and realize that you're not just getting older but that you're getting old!" For our youth goes, too. The springtime of life so quickly turns to autumn, and then to winter. In a society that idolizes youth, it's tough to accept the fact that our youth is literally wasting away.

Health and happiness? There may be some people in church this morning whose health is gone; it may never come back. Perhaps some of you are worshiping today because you are looking for healing, or your burden is too heavy to bear alone so you have come looking for a word of encouragement. For others, an increasing number of problems have cast a pall over your life, and you wish that someone would listen to you and try to understand. You are not very happy and you're not so sure you ever will be again. Life is so uncertain.

In his book, *Man's Search for Meaning,* Dr. Victor Frankl, a Jewish psychiatrist, tells how he survived three unimaginably grim years in Nazi concentration camps. His wife, his brother, his mother and father, all were killed in similar camps. He, himself, was stripped of all his possessions, all his clothing, his watch, his rings, even his glasses. Then they shaved all the hair off his body and he was utterly naked. Now, you see, the question he had to face was, "Does my life have meaning now?" Family gone; all possessions gone; position in the community, gone; all dignity, gone; possession only what he called, "My ridiculously naked life." Now does my being have roots? Is there any reason to continue living?

Well, what is it that gives meaning to a person's life? Their job? Their family? Their friends? What do you think? Or haven't you thought about it lately?

If the things in which our lives are rooted can be so easily swept away, does that mean that we are "done in?" Or, in some more tragic sense, that we are "done for?" For all of these things will go. Then what does that suggest to you? Does it say, as it did to one lady interviewed on the television show, *20/20*, that you must save all your prescription drugs and when the going gets rough, swallow them with alcohol, creating a lethal cocktail? Is that the answer?

One day, Jesus took with him the leadership of the disciples, Peter, James and John so that they might have some time to pray together. Before long Jesus would be crucified, and not long after that he would ascend to be at the right hand of God. The disciples would then be called upon to leave father and mother and family. They would be required to leave their occupations behind, and all their possessions. They would have to endure persecution and hardship; they would grow old before their time.

How could Jesus ask his disciples to do that sort of thing? To give up everything which formed the foundations of their lives? And if they accepted that challenge, where would they find the motivation for living? Where would their roots need to dig in so that they could be sustained, and draw nourishment and strength for the struggles that lay ahead?

The Bible says, "And as (Jesus) was praying, the appearance of his countenance was altered, and his raiment became dazzling white. And behold, two men talked with him, Moses and Elijah." Suddenly Peter, James, and John are given a glimpse of a reality which they never knew existed. They are overwhelmed. Was it a dream? It is too glorious for a dream. Then they hear a voice saying, "This is my Son, my Chosen; listen to him!" Listen to him. And when the voice had spoken, they looked up . . . and saw Jesus only.

Now what if Jesus was preparing his disciples for their ministry, preparing them by illustrating in this vivid way, that there are unseen realities which are far greater than the things we call "the facts of life." What if our Lord chose this method to imprint indelibly on the disciples' minds that even the greatest wonder of this world is but a dim shadow of the glory which is to come. And what if the voice was the voice of

God, and they were being taught that the greatest reality of all was Jesus Christ — only Jesus. So if they were going to make it in this world, if they were going to discover what life was meant to be, they would have to set their roots in him.

And what if that which was true for the disciples is also true for you and me? What if that which we cannot see, things like faith and hope and love, are most important to life? What if that which we often consider last is the greatest reality of all — I'm talking about God. And what if the most fundamental fact of life is really this: The Lord God omnipotent reigns! That the greatest and most important truth about every life is that it be rooted in Jesus Christ as Savior!

I suggest that nothing else will do. We need more than just a little help in this world. For the great challenges of life, your resources and mind are not adequate, to say the least. We need more than a few religious "Band-Aids" to patch up our brokenness. No ritual "first-aid" treatments can heal the grief-bruised and the soul-sick. We need God! We need God.

If we are really honest with ourselves we must admit that we are not self-sufficient. Our live is given; it is something sustained by simple things like air and food, and how easily it ends: a maladjustment of body chemistry, a too-long hesitation in the patient pumping of the heart. Our life is fragile and what is worse we often sabotage it by our own actions. It is not helpful to have holier-than-thou people point out our sins, much less to be scolded by them. Because many of us know all too well, the misery of being forsaken by the would-be gods we mistook for the Lord our God.

Simply to be told that our idols are sand which can be easily washed away is not enough, because we need to know where to set our roots. If we are dislodged, we will seek almost anything for a sense of security, even if it does not offer a solution but is only a rest area, a place to catch our breath and calm our anxiety for a bit. Our hearts rebel against being rootless and they will be attached to something, our hearts will be attached to someting. Well, let it be God!

The Bible tells us that Jesus Christ is the ground into which we are to sink our roots to draw the proper nourishment for life. Being thus faith-fed, our lives can blossom and flourish to the glory of God. And knowing that we are grounded in eternity, we can have confidence that the source of our joy will always be present to sustain us. So we put no ultimate trust, no ultimate love, no ultimate confidence in anything or anyone but Jesus Christ. Everything else is tentative — everything else is tentative!

Now I realize that that kind of theology is not popular. We'd kind of like our religion to provide a little inspiration, a little relief from this harried world. We want religion to emphasize God bringing out the best that is in us. We want to hear the message that we are really pretty good, accenting the positive, patting us on the back. The Bible keeps turning the thing around saying that faith means reckless abandonment of one's self to God, so that God may be all in all. That involves a transfiguration of life, and it's a little like asking someone to burn down his home.

One thing is sure, if it happens, it isn't going to take place just because someone made up their mind to do it. If it happens at all, it will happen because in the gospel you and I encounter Christ in such a way that we grow to depend upon him and to love him.

A funny thing happened to God on his way to earth. Nobody recognized him. They didn't think of looking in a manger, a stable, much less on a cross. To do what Jesus did for you and me reveals a love that is just a little frightening, but which also gives us a great deal of security. Now there's something to dig your roots into, something upon which to anchor your life.

The spiritual terrain of our planet Earth is not favorable for developing a depth which enables us to endure the storms and stresses of life with serenity and confidence. The superficial soils of selfishness and pleasure create a root system which skims the surface of life. Our energies are consumed in growing impressive foliage and flowers which represent all kinds of activities and trivial pursuits. But the taproot of our lives is not driven down to the depths of God. Thus we find ourselves vulnerable and unsure because our foundations are so easily shaken. You and I need to give this critical business of grounding our life at least as much time and energy as we give to the business of planning the ways in which we intend our life should blossom.

That's why we have come together, to remind each other that we have been redeemed, bought back — not with silver and gold, not with money — but with the precious body and blood of the Son of God. Therefore being redeemed by him, means that our faith and our hope, the very roots of our existence, are in God, a God in whom, "we live and move and have our being." If we do not see our Lord through the eyes of faith, we are not going to see anything else in this life clearly either.

Where have you set the roots of your life? What is the most important thing for you? If it isn't God, then what is it? What will shape and form your life if it is not God? Some of the possibilities might surprise you: what you had for breakfast and how it agreed with you. How other people treat you, especially certain people. What people say about you. How you feel. The intensity of your desires or the weight of your burdens. Who you are with. What kind of a day it is. Too often it is things like these that design our daily lives, and yet we talk about how free we are. We are not free at all until our life is rooted in Christ and our life flows forth from him.

One pastor, in talking about biblical faith, said, "The thing about Godly faith is that it is not a burden laid upon us, but rather a crown that governs us and lifts us up forever." Lifts us up above pettiness, and worry, and fear . . . and death, too. So that even when our homes and families go — and they will go, our possessions, our country, our youth, our health and our happiness — nothing will have substantially changed because our roots are still firmly embedded in the eternal fact of Jesus Christ. And our Lord says because you and I are rooted in him we will be exalted. But even that will not matter. Because the important thing, the truly important thing will not even be you or me — but that we are with Christ and that we are safe, and whole and loved . . . forever! Amen.

Lent 3
Luke 13:1-13

Planted For A Purpose

A hole is blown open in the cargo area of a 747 jumbo jet, and nine people are sucked out and killed instantly. It is natural to ask, "Why?" A tornado rips through a small community in Kansas destroying buildings and businesses which took a lifetime to establish and we grieve with them. Those are just a couple of the more spectacular of a whole series of tragic and painful events which occur daily, which trouble our hearts and create questions in our minds.

Our text this morning tells of some people who approached Jesus and asked his opinion about two incidents which raised the same questions. One apparently took place at the temple in Jerusalem, when Pilate ordered some Galileans killed while they were in the act of making animal sacrifices to God; the blood of those devout worshipers became mingled with the blood of the animals.

The other incident had happened not long before that. The tower of Siloam, which was part of the fortification of Jerusalem, had collapsed, killing 18 persons. Now the people approached Jesus and asked, "Why do those kinds of things happen?" Did they happen because the people involved were so wicked that the tragedies were God's judgment upon them?

Jesus gives no helpful explanation, he simply sidesteps the huge question of why there is pain and tragedy in the world, and he focuses instead on the purpose of human life. To him the question is not, "Why do people die the way they do?" but, "Why are we given life?"

By means of the parable of the fig tree when Jesus reminds the people of his day that Israel had a noble calling; God had planted them on earth for a particular purpose. They were to be a special people, agents of God's mercy in the world, and they were to bear fruit befitting that holy cause. In other words, instead of calling God into question and asking, "Are the misfortunes of life God's doing?" Jesus turns the tables and asks, "What are you doing in the world?" You have been called to repentance because you have not blessed others as God has blessed you.

Jesus indicates in his story that their lives have been barren, the fruits have not been forthcoming; they as a people are virtually useless to God. Yet the story has a tone of hope. Jesus recommends that things be stirred up around them, that the people be fed and the branches pruned, so that with tender care and nourishment they will blossom and produce to the glory of God.

Through this parable Jesus calls the people to renewal, to bear fruit. It is really a call to evangelize because witnessing, reminding one another of the mighty deeds of God, has always been the heart and soul of renewal. As Paul writes, "Faith comes from what is heard and what is heard comes by the preaching of Christ (Romans 10:17)."

The parable is timely for our age and for our church as well. There are many signals which indicate that the church is now at a crossroads in her life and ministry and stands in need of renewal, of inner evangelism. We need to find new ways to minister, so that the members come on Sundays to praise God, and be fed, instead of seeking alternatives to worship. We need to develop winsome methods to attract children so that greater numbers, Sunday after Sunday, experience God's grace, and feel like a part of God's family. We need to draw adults into Christian education programs so that members find fulfillment through faith in an eternal Christ, rather than in the pursuit of transient pleasures. We need to discover the key to inspiring the kind of generosity that will enable the church to be creative in developing God-pleasing ministries.

We need to take this whole matter seriously as a congregation as well, for our potential is mind boggling. Like Israel of old, our Lord is telling us today that our church, our congregation, was planted for a purpose and if we are not carrying out that purpose then it would be better if we were uprooted and destroyed. That is not very nice; it is not very comforting. But there it is, straight and to the point. The terms are established by Jesus and not by me or anyone else.

To tell the truth it makes me uncomfortable. I'd prefer to put God on the spot. Or if Jesus evades the question, as he did in our text, then I'd rather hear him speak about lilies of the field and the birds of the air, and how God takes care of them. But you and I are not lilies or birds. We're human beings, created in God's image, capable, responsible and accountable. And if we believe the Bible when it says that we are the church, then you and I are the ones to whom our Lord addresses the parable, and our mission as national church body and a congregation needs to be examined.

I suggest we begin by taking more seriously than ever before the matter of evangelism, not just out there in the world, but in here, in our own community, and specifically and intentionally within our own membership. We need to show our appreciation and need for one another, by respecting each other's gifts, by expecting something of each other, and by reaching out to those who feel unnecessary. Everyone is important, everyone is essential, everyone is beloved of God and therefore an indispensable part of our church family. We need to evangelize our own parish with that message.

Now the subject of evangelism can make us a bit uncomfortable because hearing that word can bring to mind pictures of high-powered religious crusades, revivals, and evangelists. We may wonder, "Is that what evangelism is?" We think of television preachers appealing to people to, "give their heart to Jesus," often with a subtle or maybe not to subtle assurance that if they only do that, then everything else is going to be all right, and we wonder about that.

For today, I suggest that we speak of evangelism in terms of witnessing because that is done person by person and it is the most effective tool we have in bringing about renewal. Of course, many persons have trouble with that word. Does witnessing to your faith mean buttonholing people and asking them if they're saved? Or if they've been born again? Does it mean getting on Northwest Orient Flight 585 to Minneapolis-St. Paul, and now you have 20 minutes to nail the person sitting next to you, nail him or her for the kingdom of God? Well, the Bible says we're supposed to "catch" people, so if you've got the aisle seat, then you've got the edge on them! Is that the way you do it? But isn't that a little like pulling on the flowers to make them grow? We ought to have trouble with that kind of approach. Neither our Lord nor his disciples ever dealt with anybody in that way.

Yet we are called to be evangelists, to bear witness to our faith as we live and move and have our being right here in our own community. But what does that mean? Simply, it means to tell and to be good news to other people, to bring good news into other people's lives. It's really very simple if we just let it happen, but it's also easy to get confused.

This question came up at a late night discussion of pastors some time ago, "If Jesus were to walk into this room right now, would you know him, and if so, how would you know him?" There was a long and heavy discussion, when the entire issue was turned upside down by the person who said, "The comfort, the good news of the gospel, is not that I could, would, or should know Jesus if he came into the room right now, but that he would know me!" The pastors had temporarily forgotten the wonder of God's grace: it is not we who do the holding on to, but it is we who are held.

That is the witness we are to share with one another and with the world, the good news that we are saved because Jesus Christ died for us and offers salvation full and free and we are held in his marvelous power and love. It is as simple as that, yet as profound and rich and deep.

When people are approached about the matter of witnessing they often say they feel inferior. They don't think you should barge into a person's life and bombard them with your witness. I think they are right. So how does one go about it?

When we share the good news with other people, we are not to go around buttonholing them — we are not to hammer them with the gospel. We try to do what God would do. And what did God do? God became incarnate, he became present with us. So we are to be present with one another, to come to them in love. That is the setting, that's the atmosphere of witnessing, to above all else, care for others and illustrate it by treating them compassionately.

We need, of course, to be encouraged to read God's Word so that we can share it. In fact, there is no better way to grow in faith than by letting God speak to you through the Bible. But like all good news it has to get out, it needs to be shared. Like a lake which requires that water flow through it to retain its fresh, life-giving properties, so faith retains its vitality and strength by flowing out into the world to share its power by treating people carefully, with maturity, respect, appreciation, and love. The truths of Scripture are best understood when one sees them embodied in another person.

Somehow we've got to find a way to illustrate to the unchurched in our community and to our own members who are as yet uninvolved, that our congregation cares. We want them to hear God's word because it is liberating and life-giving, and it will open their hearts to experience the goodness and mercy of God. But it must be born out of genuine concern.

There's a story of a nurse who gave unselfish and devoted care to her patients. One man was deeply moved and thanked the nurse gratefully. The nurse replied, "O, I'm not doing it for you; I'm doing it for Jesus." How would you feel if you were the patient? Sounds good, sounds religious, sounds pious — it's just awful! We are to be present for one another with compassion and respect.

That orientation toward people has all kinds of things to say about how we run a congregation. It has an impact on everything we do, from our stewardship program, to our youth activities, to how we receive new members, to how we operate in our organizations, committees and council. Our church should be a fellowship in which the good news is not only "on going" but, as someone has said, "where it is also going on." All that we do should reflect God's unconditional invitation to experience the gospel, the good news. That is why we cannot simply stand by and let our brothers and sisters in Christ, young and old, drift away from the power and the glory of the gospel. We must all be witnesses. We are compelled by the gospel to call one another back into the family and to speak words of acceptance, and to invite them to participate in the activities of the family because then, and only then, can they experience the warmth and joy of what it means to be God's people.

I hope you begin to see how very important it is, not only that we belong to this congregation, but that we participate in its congregational life. We are planted for a purpose, to bear fruit that members, old and new, might be drawn in to receive the gifts of God and that they in turn might become gracious gifts to God and to us. We are to be a fellowship of believers who live bearing God's creative, liberating word to all the world.

So our purpose as a faithful people of God is not to give answers to all the questions of life; our cause is evangelism — in our community and out into the world. And as we are faithful, our church, our congregation will bear fruits befitting a people who have been saved by God's amazing grace. The implications are tremendous, for as we carry out our mission, we will receive more members, and we will need space for them, and we will need personnel to minister to them. Surely it will create problems, surely it will be a challenge, but we have no choice in the matter, because like the disciples of old, Jesus calls us to be fishers of people, not merely keepers of the aquarium. So we commit ourselves to sharing the good news, in the name of Christ, to stir things up, to nourish the people of God, to open our arms to be blessed by the glory of God. If we are faithful, we will be blessed, because that's God's promise, and that's the way it will be. Amen.

Lent 4
Luke 15:11-24

The Story Of The Scandalized Neighbors

I don't know what this world is coming to. It seems to me that parents don't do as good a job raising their kids as they used to. Consider my neighbor. His punk kid ran off with a wad of money last year. A couple of days ago he came back looking like death warmed over and what are they doing? They're throwing a party for him. From what I've heard they are going to spend a bundle on it. Sounds like the affair will be bigger than a wedding bash. If you ask me it's scandalous, celebrating as though he was a wonderful, long lost loved one returned. It is tough raising kids these days and they are setting a poor example for the rest of us. But let me tell the story from the beginning.

My name is Aaron. I live on a farm across the road from Eli and Rachel Kahal. They're a devout Jewish couple, no doubt about it, but from my point of view they have always been too lax on discipline, especially when it came to their youngest son, Judah. He was trouble from the day he was born. I've often wondered how a rascal like that could come from such a good family. He would rob me of figs, scare my sheep — you know, all the nasty little things young boys do to aggravate people. Quite a contrast from his brother Amos. Now he is a decent fellow; works hard, goes to the synagogue regularly, respects his parents and his neighbors! There ought to be more kids like him.

In any case, it didn't surprise me when I heard that young Judah had asked his father for the inheritance due him so he could leave town. Gossip has it that Eli was so stunned that he didn't even try to talk the boy out of it. I know what I would do if one of my sons came up to me and said, by implication,

"I wish you were dead so I could get my hands on the inheritance." The thought of it would break a mother's heart! I would have given the kid nothing but a swift kick and tossed him out on his ear.

Maybe you don't know that in our culture when a son asked for his inheritance he was asking to be cut off from his family forever. In fact, the family would grieve as though he had died and, from that point on, he would always be referred to in the past tense. It wasn't merely a matter of running away from home.

Contrary to public opinion, I'm sure Eli tried to talk him out of it even though Judah did very little around the farm and was more trouble than help. But it was no use, the lad was probably tired of being hassled by everyone so, determined to free himself from the last ties to common sense, he took off for the big city.

It was the best thing that ever happened to the rumor mill in our community! I'll tell you the whole affair set tongues to wagging like you wouldn't believe, and it got even better. The tales which came back to our little town whenever anyone went to the big city were staggering. It seems Judah made quite a name for himself as a big spender. BMWs, wild parties, lots of women, booze and drugs. Some of the more religious people were sure he would die of AIDS. Of course none of us knew how much of it was true, but it sure wasn't hard to believe. In any case, it was clear that young Judah, out there in the "far country" as we called it, had not only turned his back on his family but that he had forsaken all moral values as well.

It was hard on the whole family but his father Eli was particularly pathetic. Often he would go out to the gate and, with haggard face and longing eyes, strain to see some sign of that lost son of his coming down the road. He tried hard to hide the tears which would well up inside him but everyone knew of the anguish, even if they could not understand. As you might guess, resentment in our town continued to grow toward the boy. We all agreed that Eli and Rachel were much better off without Judah. At least they could sleep at night, not having to wonder where he was or what he was doing, or if they would have to go to the hospital or the jail to pick him up, as they so often did when he lived at home.

Judah, however, was not better off without his family. As I heard the story, It hadn't taken him long to run through his inheritance, so he had to get a job. Unfortunately he hadn't felt it important to learn a trade so there wasn't much he could do. Even worse, the economy took a dive and suddenly he found himself without cash, without housing, without a job and without food. His old friends out there in the "far country" didn't want anything to do with him. You can tolerate a leech for only so long. He had tried to buy friends with his money but had only purchased their scorn.

Finally Judah found a farmer and offered to watch over his pigs. Now that may not seem particularly strange to you, but it sure sent shock waves through our little town when we heard of it. Just think! tending pigs, the most unclean of all animals. To our Jewish way of thinking he had finally sunk into the gutter. Not only had he turned his back on his family and renounced all moral values, now he had rejected God and cut himself off from his Hebrew heritage. He brought shame upon us all!

Let me try to put it in terms you can understand. How would you react if a boy who came from a respected family of your church denied his Christianity, his American citizenship and his cultural heritage all in one act? I tell you, there were many who were so angered by Judah's actions that they even stopped feeling sorry for his parents, as much as they liked them.

It is a fact of life, once you've turned away from everything that speaks of commitment and love, once you have abandoned all that is good and decent, once you have denied all that is sacred and holy, life is going to cave in on you. It did for Judah. Out there tending the swine he got so hungry he was willing to eat pigslop. The only good thing is that without money he was unable to buy booze or drugs to mess up his mind. So while he sat there sick of body, sick at heart and sick of soul, he began to think.

Being a smart boy, it eventually dawned on him that his father's servants were warm while he was cold, they were feasting on food while he was starving to death. They enjoyed the sweetness of fellowship on the family farm while he suffered the pain of loneliness.

He must have wrestled with the method he would use to get himself back onto his father's farm. He had rejected everything his parents held dear, but I would guess, knowing this father had always been soft of heart and easily persuaded, he decided to say, "Father, I have sinned against heaven and before you."

Now let me interject. We Jews have often, and for good reason, been accused of exaggerating. But I tell you, we are also gifted at understatement. That young scoundrel had not merely sinned against heaven and against Eli, he had violated every law and abused every relationship he ever had. In truth, he had offended everyone. Everyone!

"Father," he said, I suppose because it would really tug on Eli's heartstrings, "I have sinned against heaven and before you; I am no longer worthy to be called your son." Worthy! He had no worth! He had long ago turned his back on sonship and asked to be considered as a dead man. He had trampled on everything his father held in reverence. How dare he appeal to his father's sensibilities in that way. I suppose he dared because he was desperate, and he knew his father, he knew his father's love, his hopes and dreams and so he used Eli's strength against him in this way.

"Father, I have sinned against heaven and before you; I am no longer worthy to be called your son; treat me as one of your hired servants." It was not a long speech, easily rehearsed and remembered as he stumbled his way back to the community and family he had so blithely renounced. I'm sure he knew it would be effective. He must have smiled and thought, "Tonight I will eat and find rest in the warmth and comfort of the servants' quarters."

You know what happened next. That fool father was out there looking for him, as was his custom every day. Only this day was different. This day he saw against the horizon the stooped form of a man hobbling down the road. Instinctively he sensed it was his son and he ran to him, the pain in his heart was transformed into compassion. Judah stopped. He wanted to run but he was frozen with fear. You see, he wasn't sure of the emotional state of the old man who ran toward him. He was comforted a bit by the fact that he still remembered his "speech." But before he could utter the words, Eli embraced him and kissed him. Feeling the strong heartbeat of his father's love, Judah collapsed into his arms and their tears intermingled in the absolution of grace.

Still Judah felt a need to say it, to give his speech, and so he blurted out his well-worn words, "Father, I have sinned against heaven and before you; I am no longer worthy to be called your son." But the father was past needing a confession, he cut him off, saying, "Quickly, bring out a robe — the finest one — and put it on him; put a ring on his finger and sandals on his feet. And get the fatted calf and kill it, and let us eat and celebrate; for this son of mine was dead and is alive again; he was lost and is found."

Let me tell you, the townsfolk did not share the joy of Eli and Rachel, not at all. We simply did not believe that Judah should have been bestowed with all the signs of sonship and authority, at least not without some kind of probationary period. I speak for all of them when I say this is the way that the homecoming should have gone:

Then Eli saw the wayward boy coming and waited for him to get to the gate of the family home. He stood there with his hands on his hips glaring at Judah until he withered before him and dared not say a word. So the father was the first to speak. "I knew you would come crawling back. Do you have any idea of what you have done to us, your mother and me? You have brought shame on us all. You don't even deserve to stand there. But, because I am a compassionate man, your mother and I have decided to take you back with a couple of provisions. First, you will go make sacrifice for your sins and you will attend worship every Sabbath without fail. You will, without complaint, follow the rules of our home. It's about time you started leading a decent life. Finally, your brother Amos is now in charge of the farm. You do what he tells you or out you go. Do you understand?"

Judah, rightly reprimanded, meekly agreed to the demands and settled down to live a quiet, productive, God-fearing life from that day forward. That's the way I think it should have been: no party, no celebration, no big deal. That just makes sense.

But there was a party, and such a party as my wife and I had never seen before. Since we had been life-long neighbors we felt obligated to attend. Besides we were more than a little curious about the wayward boy and what he had been up to. We felt sorry for Judah's brother Amos, because in our memory we could never think of a time when Eli and Rachel had done anything like this for him, and he was such a nice young man, too. We did not blame Amos for not showing up. In fact, there were quite a number of people from our community who were so scandalized by the whole affair that they refused to attend, in spite of their affection for Rachel and Eli.

We were surprised, however, to meet Judah. Here was no brash young man; gone were the arrogant and flippant airs to which we had become accustomed. He appeared to be a person who was at peace with himself and there glowed from his eyes a warmth and sincerity which impressed even me. Humble he went about the room and, with tears in his eyes, apologized for what he had done. I was thunderstruck, and must admit that I was touched by his display of courage and humility.

I had never witnessed the conversion of a person before, so I was unprepared for its power and beauty. Whatever else that evening meant for those who attended, it certainly captured the wonder, joy and grace of the remarkable change in Judah's life. Now I feel badly that Amos did not become a part of it.

One thing still gnaws at me. While it is difficult for me to approve of the way Eli received back his rebellious son, I am convinced that it was not the tragedy in the far country that changed Judah, it was the tenacious and shameless love of Eli and Rachel. The undeserved love of his parents gave Judah the strength, security and desire to return and, in turn, transfigured his life. Scandalized as I am by such an unmerited and lavish outpouring of affection and acceptance, if I had in foolishness followed the path into the far country, I would want a father — no, I would need a father like Eli. Looking at him that night I envied him for I could sense that he had experienced more joy in his heart that day than I had known in my entire life. Then it occurred to me, "Surely that is why there is so much joy in heaven when a sinner repents and why the Heavenly Father's heart overflows in ecstasy each time that you or I return."

Lent 5
John 8:1-11 [RC]
John 12:1-8 [C]
Luke 20:9-14 [L]

Two R-Rated Stories

We are going to look at two R-rated stories from the life of Christ this morning. I use the term "R-rated" in the sense that when some people observed the behavior of Jesus in these events, they were so morally incensed that in each case they felt he should be censured.

The opening scene of the first story begins with a woman who had been dragged out of her house by a couple of her pastors; they had not even given her time to comb her hair or properly dress. She had been caught red-handed, found committing adultery by her husband. He had immediately notified the church in order that justice might be served, because according to Jewish law any woman who committed adultery was to be stoned to death.

You can imagine the crowd that gathered around as this pious parade of pharisees ushered the shame-faced woman through the streets of her village.

How do you suppose they treated her, the hometown folk? Can you imagine it would be any different than when scandals break loose in our own communities? Whispers and accusations abounded, "opportunist, home-wrecker, whore" — who knows all the names with which she was pummeled as she was led through the streets? And where was the man, the partner in her sexual alliance? Why wasn't he there? Why was he not brought with her to be shriveled by their self-righteous condemnation? Apparently there were two standards in operation at the time, one for women and one for men; not so different from today.

In any case, the priests decided that the woman would be a test case to check on the moral values of the teacher, Jesus from Nazareth. They heard that he was soft on sinners, that he sat and ate with them, that he befriended them and offered them love and forgiveness. "What will this world become," thought the pastors, "if the laws against sin are not upheld, if sinful behavior is not punished." So with grim determination they charged through the city with the convicted woman in tow. Suddenly they appeared before a startled Jesus. "Rabbi," they say, "this married woman was found in another man's bed. You know the law of Moses says she deserves to be stoned to death for her adultery. What do you say about her?"

The trap has been set; the bait is deliciously scandalous; there was no way the Rabbi could escape. If he said, "let the woman go," the people would see that he disregarded the laws of Moses and could not be taken seriously. If he said, "Go ahead and stone her," he would be seen as a man without mercy and as one who violated his own words of love and forgiveness.

For a long time Jesus knelt, deep in thought, and wrote with his finger on the ground. In fact, he took so much time that the priests became impatient and demanded an answer from him. Finally he said, "You are right. According to the law of Moses she deserves to be killed. Go ahead and stone her if you must, but let the first stone be thrown by someone who is without sin."

And then the Bible says, "When they heard it, they went away, one by one, and Jesus was left alone with the woman standing before him." Can you imagine how she felt? What relief? What gratitude? What admiration?

I would guess most of us can not, but I remember a young lady not unlike the woman in our text who came to me one day, overcome with guilt and shame. When she was finally able to break through the barriers of self-reproach she experienced the wonder of forgiveness; she cried, then laughed, and then she smiled and said, "I feel giddy, like when I was a teenager."

That's what forgiveness does for a person. It creates an atmosphere in which the sparkling bubbles of hope and faith and love begin to rise in one's soul. That's why the confession and absolution at the beginning of worship is my favorite part. I love to hear the words of forgiveness and freedom over and over. I am saddened when I go to worship conferences and hear workshop leaders say that the "Order for Confession and Absolution" should be omitted from our worship on festival Sundays because of its mood-dampening effect. I wonder if those leaders have ever really experienced or understood the magnificence of forgiveness as Paul, or the woman in our text, or as I have. If they had, they could never see it as anything but life-restoring, uplifting, exhilarating and joyful.

Jesus senses the release and ecstasy in the woman's heart as she stands before him. He can see it in her eyes, so he asked, "Has no one condemned you?" She said, "No one, Lord." And Jesus said, "Neither do I condemn you; go, and do not sin again."

Well, do you suppose he really meant that, "Go and sin no more." That seems like a rather impossible challenge! I believe rather that Jesus was saying to the woman that he believed in her, believed that her life could be different. The circumstances which had brought her to that moment were not immutable, they could be changed. Jesus was granting her power and permission to live out her life in righteousness and joy. She needed to understand that it is not God's will that she be humiliated by remorse. Jesus showed her that God is not a sadistic being who enjoys seeing his children in mental agony squirming on the rack of guilt. God, who is love incarnate, identifies with the sinner and offers the option of restoration and forgiveness.

We need to practice what Jesus preached and let people live in that restoration, that forgiveness. The story of Lily as told by Fran Burnford who was an assistant to the bishop of the Southern Pacific District in the ALC is a wonderful example.

"Lily began attending our church when we 10-year-old girls were in a Sunday school class and we asked our teacher and other adults why they referred to Lily as the woman of sin?

"Certainly we knew that Lily looked different from all the other women of our congregation. She wore high-heels and lipstick; she was by far the prettiest woman we'd ever seen. 'Woman of sin,' what did it mean?

"In our Illustrated King James Version of the Bible there was a picture on page 90 with the caption, 'Woman of Sin anoints the feet of Jesus.' We studied that picture looking for clues. There were five figures in the scene. The three men who stood in the background glaring furiously looked a bit like the Elders at our local Baptist church. The glare on the faces was just like the one they used when they stood at the end of the pews during communion to make sure that the children didn't snitch any bread. It was the same glare that they had on their faces whenever Lily came into church and sat by herself and wasn't even offered communion.

"Then there was Jesus in the picture: blonde, blue-eyed, wearing a dazzling white robe, a shining halo around his head, his hand resting tenderly on the head of the 'woman of sin,' who knelt weeping at his feet.

"The 'woman of sin' wore a crimson robe which was only a little deeper red than her hair which flowed at least down to her waist. She looked exactly like Rita Hayworth who we had only seen in magazines because we weren't allowed to attend the movies.

" 'Woman of sin.' What was her sin? Playing 'Woman of sin' became a favorite pretend game for us girls. We'd imagine the worst, most shocking scenario we could. Something that would really offend the elders at the local church. Our favorite scenarios were: that Lily had been seen coming out of a movie, or maybe the Saturday night dance. Or maybe Lily had been seen smoking or coming out of the state controlled liquor store with a brown bag.

"Would Lily ever publicly confess her sins at the Thursday night prayer meetings? Attendance escalated in hopeful anticipation. Lily did stand up every Thursday and speak, 'By grace I have received forgiveness for my sins. I thank God for giving me new life.' Then she would sit down and say no more.

"Then one Sunday morning Lily stood up in the pew and walked clear down the center aisle to the front of the church, she turned around and faced the congregation and said in a clear voice, 'I'm leaving this church to find another church where people will rejoice with me in God's forgiving grace. You people only want to wallow in my old life. You don't see that I'm a new person.' And out of the church she walked and never returned.

"The next Sunday was communion Sunday. Three 10-year-old girls carried out a pact that they had made secretly during the week. Under the furious glare of the elders each one of them took not one, but two pieces of communion bread, one for themselves and one for Lily. Though we didn't know what to call it, she had given us our first glimpse of freedom, of newness in Christ. Somehow as young as we were we understood that it was Lily's faith, her new life, that angered and frightened that congregation so much more than her sin."

We know that the Holy Spirit is continually at work restoring, reshaping and giving new life to his people just like he did in Lily's life and the lives of three 10-year-old girls.

It is important that we as God's people permit others to live their new life and not keep bringing up their past. We acknowledge, by our kindness, that God does indeed change people and we join them in glorifying God for the miracle that has taken place in their life.

Sometimes the change which comes over people when the Holy Spirit is working within them challenges the values of others. This is illustrated in a second "R-rated" story which involves Jesus. The event takes place in the home of Mary, Martha and Lazarus (the one whom Jesus would one day raise from the dead). Overwhelmed with gratitude and awe, Mary anoints the feet of Jesus with a pound of costly ointment. In an act of devotion and appreciation she does not rise but kneels and pours the perfume over Jesus' feet. If she had had a ring of diamonds and rubies that would no doubt have been her gift. She did not have jewelry, so she gave that which was most precious to her and poured it out upon him. That is the nature of true faith — it always seeks a way to give and to share, to express thankfulness for the amazing gifts of God.

That kind of seemingly wasteful liberality is always disturbing, especially to those who have not been liberated to enjoy the winsome and serendipitous nature of our God. Judas was one of those persons. He always seemed so deadly serious. Everything had to be purposeful and on the outside he seemed to have his priorities straight. "Hey!" he says, "that ointment could have been sold for hundreds of dollars and given to the poor. What a waste pouring it over the Master's feet."

Judas had a cause and it is sometimes hard for people who champion causes to be able to let their gifts, their wealth, be freed for celebration as well as helping. Indeed, as in Judas' case, his supposed concern for the cause of the poor, prevented him from enjoying Mary's ministry to Jesus. To him it seemed frivolous; to Jesus it meant a great deal.

A similar incident happened at a church recently. When the congregation built their new worship center the old organ, a small electronic model, was transferred into the new sanctuary; clearly it was inadequate but finances were tight. Then one day one of the wealthier members announced he thought they needed a new organ and would contribute $100,000 toward its installation. Instantly one of the "pillars of the church" who had opposed the building project from the beginning denounced him for such wastefulness, "With the thousands of people who are dying from hunger each day," he said, "the money should be given to world hunger." The donor responded, "You give your $100,000 to world hunger; I'll give mine for the organ. I seem to remember that Jesus said we are to use 'unrighteous mammon' to glorify God. I think the building of this church and the organ will do that."

Another problem with being cause-centered is that while it may seem righteous, people can easily lose their focus. I remember back in 1966 when I was on crutches because of an accident, a seminary classmate came rushing up to me and said, "We're going to march on the state capital building in solidarity with the blacks in Atlanta. Will you join us? We think it would be good to have you on crutches." I refused but added, "if you ever march in protest of how blacks are being treated in North Minneapolis, let me know, I'll lead the parade." Sometimes a cause "out there" can be used as an excuse to keep from getting involved in ministry that needs to be carried out "right here."

I like what Madeleine L'Engle says about this matter: "I watch in horror as a great liberal, passionately interested in the cause of — shall we say — the leper, very carefully avoids speaking to the leper in his path, in order to get on with the cause. And it occurs to me that Jesus couldn't have cared less about the cause of the leper or the rights of the leper. But when there was a leper in his path he did not walk abound him like the priest walking on the opposite side of the road from the man set upon by thieves, on his way to Jerusalem to preach his famous sermon on compassion. Jesus stopped. And healed. And loved. Not causes, but people."[1]

Jesus said to Judas, "The poor you always have with you, but you do not always have me." It was not that our Lord was against helping the poor, but he was saying that there are times when giving to other projects is as expedient or perhaps even more appropriate. Certainly supporting the congregation's efforts to minister to the poor in heart and spirit is at least as important as reaching out to the financially poor. In our parish we need the generosity of many Marys to carry out the far-reaching programs and ministries which God has called us to do in this time and place.

Jesus' obvious pleasure at receiving Mary's lavish gift gives us a clue as to God's appreciation for sacrificial giving. One's giving always reflects one's faith.

Sometimes I have heard it said that the church is only interested in money. In my experience that is most certainly untrue! From our story we see that Jesus was obviously pleased at Mary's lavish gift, not because he was impressed with its value, but because it reflected the sacrificial quality of her faith. One's giving, whether time, energy or money, is always a mark of faith. It is true, the church, like all other organizations, needs money to exist and carry out the mission, but our primary goal is the restoration of people to Jesus Christ and not financial security.

It can take some time for us to understand that truth. I recall the witness of Professor Fred Craddock who wrote, "When I was growing up in North Tennessee, my father didn't go to church. He was at home fussing about lunch being late on Sunday. Once in a while the pastor would come and try to talk to him, but he was kind of rough on the minister. He would say, 'I know what you fellows want down there at the church. You want another name and another pledge. Right? Isn't that the business you're in? Another name and another pledge.' It embarrassed my mother. She would stay in the kitchen and cry. Once in a while they would have a guest evangelist and he would come with the pastor and the pastor would say, 'Here is the toughie, see him!' My father would always say something like, 'You don't care about me. You want another member, another pledge. That is how the churches operate. You don't care about me.' He said it, I guess, a thousand times. One time he didn't say it. It was in a veterans' hospital. I rushed across the country to see him. He was down to 74 pounds. They had taken out his throat but they said it was too late. All that radium stuff had just burned him to pieces. They put in a tube so he could breathe but he couldn't speak. I looked around the room. In the windows, on the tables, flowers — cut flowers and potted plants — even that table that they swing out over your bed to put food on had flowers on it. He couldn't eat. I looked at the little cards sprinkled in all the flowers and almost every one of them — men's group, women's fellowship, pastor, others at church, nearly every one of them, the flowers and the deep stack of cards stacked beside the flowers — from persons and groups within that church.

"He saw me look at those cards. He took a pencil and wrote on the side of a Kleenex box a line from Hamlet, 'In this harsh world, draw your breath in pain, to tell my story.'

"I asked, 'What is your story dad?' And he wrote a confession: 'I was wrong!' "[2]

We as a church are interested in persons, not causes. We are committed to introducing people to Jesus Christ, not merely adding people to our membership list. We are more concerned with the contributions of our members to the kingdom of God than we are with their gifts to the congregation's budget, but sometimes it is hard to distinguish between the two. For when we come to experience the absolute forgiveness, love and acceptance of God as the woman taken in adultery did, we are moved to respond with the kind of liberality characterized by Mary's act of love; the two tales are intertwined.

So I encourage you to come and find forgiveness and peace with God. I invite you as well to find ways to express your gratitude. Both these acts are expressions of faith which create the joy and fulfillment so characteristic of the Christian life. Go now into the world knowing that you are forgiven, loved, accepted and appreciated. In the name of Jesus Christ you are. God bless your week. Amen.

---

1. L'Engle, Madeleine. *The Irrational Season.* Harper and Row, Publishers, San Francisco, 1977. p. 138.

2. *Pulpit Resource,* Vol. 9, No. 4, 1981. pp. 32-33.

Passion/Palm Sunday
Luke 19:28-40

That's Our God For You!

Palm Sunday is an event in Christ's life that many people, particularly young people, enjoy. It is action packed, filled with lots of commotion and noise — especially noise. It centers around a grand parade with all the excitement and frenzied emotion of a political convention. The "Triumphant Entry into Jerusalem," as it is sometimes called, includes people lining the streets craning their necks to see, waving palms, and lots of shouting. For many people who like lots of activity, Palm Sunday is their kind of festival. It provides plenty of action.

Actions are important because through them we learn about people. We say, "Actions speak louder than words," because we are not always what we appear to be. We reveal ourselves, little by little through how we act and react; by what we do. That is also how we get to know God. We can ask all kinds of questions about God, but how can we get the answers? How will we ever get to know what God is like? The Bible says God is an invisible Spirit, and we will never get a glimpse of God's nature until we first examine what he has done.

When God became human in Jesus of Nazareth, that opened up new possibilities for understanding God, of getting to know what God is like. After all, we come to know and enjoy each other through our responses; we illustrate who we are by what we do.

The story is told of a little boy, Billy. He visited his grandmother in California one summer and almost wore her out with his vigorous activity. She was accustomed to living a peaceful, orderly life. He was perpetual motion, into everything. One might when they were both sound asleep, there was an earthquake. The grandmother was awakened by the house shaking and in her concern called out, "Billy, Billy!" To which came the response, "I didn't do it, grandma!" Well, Billy was a little like an earthquake at times to a grandma who liked her quiet lifestyle.

It is by our reactions that we reveal ourselves day by day and so are known by one another. It is by our interactions with others that we paint, stroke by stroke, the portrait of who we are.

In the events preceding and following the Palm Sunday entry into Jerusalem, the actions of Jesus speak volumes. Knowing that suffering and death lay ahead of him if he went to Jerusalem, he resolutely charted his course to be there during the Passover celebration.

Jesus could have played it safe. If he valued his life he should have entered Jerusalem by night and slipped in on the back streets until he reached secure shelter. But our Lord entered the city in a way that deliberately set himself on the stage and intentionally riveted every eye upon himself. He purposely challenged the religious and political power-brokers of the day by riding into town like a king, as the one in charge. That is the impression he wanted to give us and that was, in fact, the truth. From that time on, no matter how things may have looked to the casual observer, Jesus was still in control.

In other words, the Jesus that the gospels portray is not a poor, well-meaning, but unfortunate teacher who got caught up in a series of ill-fated events. The drama of Holy Week is neither random nor accidental. In each circumstance we see that our Lord is in control. He is in control of himself and he's in control of what happens. He, not his captors. Let's look at it.

In the garden that fateful Friday night when Judas kissed him, Jesus asked, "Friend, for what purpose have you come?" Jesus knew Judas was there for a reason; the betrayal comes as no surprise. In fact he had spoken about it at supper. It is clear that the betrayed was sovereign over the betrayer.

As the scene continued, it was the captive who seemed to be most free. He did not condone violent action; he would not be party to it. He didn't ask for 100 legions of angels to come and deliver him from the situation because he came to that hour for that purpose. Nor did he allow the disciples to take up arms and fight for him. When Peter grabbed his sword and began to do battle, Jesus rebuked him saying, "Those who live by the sword will die by the sword." Once order was restored, Jesus quietly, and without protest, led the soldiers back into town where he would be charged and booked. Jesus revealed by what he did that he was in command all the way.

This, too, is significant. At one point in the story the leaders of the Jews are gathered together in unanimous agreement that they must not put Jesus to death during the Passover festival because they feared the reaction of the people. At that very time, Jesus was telling his disciples that he would die during the celebration of the Passover — and of course he did. Jesus was in charge.

Our Lord's majestic silence before both Pilate and Herod suggests that he was the one in command. That was his moment, his time. The sufferings at the hands of the soldiers represented the purpose for which he had come. He had chosen the plan for the salvation of the world and it would be carried out even though Pilate tried in many ways to release him.

So Jesus didn't come into Jerusalem looking much like a king. He didn't act much like we think a king should act — and he doesn't even today because he still comes to us, not as one who takes, but as one who gives, not as one who is served but as one who serves. Jesus gives himself up in love to his subjects which is not at all the way kings normally act.

Now we can be fooled by all of this, underestimating who Christ really is. So we tend to devotionalize him, make him the object of thimble-thin piety. Jesus can become a "king of hearts," a source of emotional highs, rather than a source of strength for deliberate cross-bearing. So we say some strange things like "we take Jesus along with us wherever we go," as though God tagged along behind us only at our request, forgetting that he promised that he is with us always — always. That he is never far from us.

The amazing thing is that he lets us get away with all that! He even gives us the unbelievable freedom to say, "No!" to him and to his lordship. That's because he loves us so much he will not twist our arms until we agree to obey him, nor will he force us into his loving, forgiving arms.

However, through Jesus Christ, a new bit of graffiti has been etched on the walls of the universe. It is the bold fact intended for all, both great and not-so-great, who would stand against him and it is this: Christ is King; he is in charge. That's the way it is. And that's the way it will always be.

Often, as in the Palm Sunday events, he doesn't look much like a monarch, but don't let appearances fool you. Christ is Lord of all and he will reign for ever and ever. He is King of kings and of him, the Bible says, "God has highly exalted him and has given him the name that is above every name, so that at the name of Jesus every knee should bend in heaven and on earth every tongue should confess that Jesus Christ is Lord of all (Philippians 2:9-11)." We are to make no mistake about that!

On Marco Polo's celebrated trip to the Orient, he was taken before the great and fearsome ruler, Genghis Khan. Now what was Marco Polo supposed to do before this mighty pagan conqueror? One false move could cost him his life. He decided to tell the story of Jesus as it is recorded in the gospels. It is said that when Marco Polo related the events of Holy Week, and described Jesus' betrayal, his trial, his scourging and crucifixion, Genghis Khan became more and more agitated, more engrossed in the story, and more tense. When Marco Polo pronounced the words, "Then Jesus bowed his head and yielded up his spirit," Genghis Khan could no longer contain himself. He interrupted, bellowing, "What did the Christian's God do then? Did he send thousands of angels from heaven to smite and destroy those who killed his Son?"

What did the Christian's God do then? He watched his beloved Son die, that's what the Christian's God did then. For that was the way Jesus chose to ascend the throne of his kingdom and to establish his Lordship for all time. Not at all the way we would expect God to demonstrate his might and power, but that's the way it was and that is how we know what our God is like.

In practical terms that means that this suffering King, who rules in love, comes to lay his claim on your life. Your entire life, is subject to his Lordship, not just a portion of it. Dr. Alvin N. Rogness, president emeritus of Luther-Northwestern Seminary explained it this way, "This means that we have to do more than shout a few hosannas or sing a few songs in praise of him. It must mean more than setting aside an hour a week to honor him, or parting with a generous offering to advance his cause. It means that, to be sure, but much more. To have Christ be our King means that we rely on him for everything, most of all the forgiveness of sins. It means being ushered into the Father's great family. It means living day by day in the Father's house and doing things the way the Father wants them done."

That's good news for you and me because living in harmony with God keeps us in touch with the day by day unfolding of our Lord's love. There is so much bad news in the world that we can be overwhelmed until we begin to wonder if God really is in charge. Only in continually experiencing God's divine love do we grow rich in our understanding of what God is like.

The story is told of an American soldier who had drawn remote duty and had written home to his wife, telling her of his seven new friends with whom he had developed a close friendship. "I am so grateful," he said, "because in this isolated and barren land a person could easily be driven to despair." When his next birthday rolled around, there was a large package in the mail from the States. When he opened it, he discovered not one gift, but eight gifts. One for him and one for each of his seven friends. The soldier looked at the eight presents and, with tears rolling down his cheeks, exclaimed, "That's my wife for you! Yes sir, that's my wife!"

The wife was revealed by her actions. That was the kind of thing she would do. That was her nature. That's what she was like. Today, as we pause at the doorway of Holy Week, we look at the cross and we recall the whole story of pain, suffering, darkness and death. And as we gaze upon our King, arms spread wide in forgiving love, we proclaim, "That's our God for you! Yes, that's what our God is like! Amen."

Maundy Thursday
Luke 22:7-20 [C, L]
John 13:1-15 [RC]

Portrait Of A Powerful Servant

Jesus loved to paint portraits for the soul. He did it through his actions as well as his words. Indeed, his whole life was a powerful illustration. On the particular night to which our texts bear witness, the image Jesus will etch into the memories of his disciples will be so powerful that they will never again be able to think of him without reference to this event.

Writer Walter Wangerin suggests that the atmosphere of that evening was shrouded in mystery and filled with intrigue. There was the meal held in secret, the carefully plotted plan: "Listen," the householder said, "let's use a signal. I'll send a man with a jar of water through the city." (Usually women carried jars of water, while men bore wineskins.) "Have your disciples follow him. No words. No talk. I'll furnish the upper room."[1]

The stage was set. The time was ripe. One by one the disciples came, trudging along dusty streets to celebrate the Passover with Jesus; it was to be their last supper with him. They entered the house and waited for the Lord to come. As they sat there they began to quarrel over which of them would be the greatest in the kingdom that Jesus, the Messiah, would establish. They wondered where in the cabinet each might be placed. Who would be in the positions of greatest power? Who would have the Messiah's ear at the time of political or religious crisis? Each had reasons for assuming that he would play a major role. Certainly the enthusiastic demonstration of the people which accompanied Jesus' entry into Jerusalem would thrust Jesus into the political forefront and initiate the coming of his kingdom.

The discussion apparently prevented them from carrying out the foot-cleansing which one usually engaged in upon entering a home. And because the roads were dirt, and people wore sandals, everyone who came into a house entered with filthy feet.

Normally a servant (the lowliest person on the staff) was assigned the dismal duty of removing the sandals and washing the feet of each one who arrived. The disciples, seeing that there was no one present to carry out the task, knew that they should take turns at that wretched job — but nobody moved. They all sat there with grimy feet, glaring at each other and jabbering about who was most important. Nobody took the basin and no one reached for a towel. Each one, wanting to be served, refused to stoop and wash another's feet.

So they sat, self-satisfied and sullen, until Jesus came. Then he, who truly was the greatest, the One unto whom all power on heaven and earth had been given, humbled himself. His hands gripped the basin and the towel and he calmly and lovingly began to wash their feet. The silence screamed in their ears as Jesus went from disciple to disciple. Shamed and shocked they watched as their Lord carried out that menial task. In this act, Christ became the servant. Imagine! God on his knees because of the arrogance of the disciples. Do you suppose they would ever forget that image?

When he finished, he said to them: "Do you understand what I have just done for you?" The disciples must have nodded their collective heads but, understanding it was beyond them. Jesus went on, "You call me 'Teacher' and 'Lord,' and rightly so, for that is what I am. Now I, your Lord and Teacher, have set you an example that you should do as I have done for you."

Jesus was not suggesting that they go about the countryside washing people's feet. That misses the point. Indeed, the modern custom of foot-washing is a mere practice of piety because it is an anachronism, a once useful practice which is no longer appropriate. Jesus did not deal in mere symbols. He did what needed to be done and did not observe customs and rituals for their own sake. The example Jesus burned into the memories of his disciples was the portrait of a servant. He wanted them to know that the highest calling in life is not to be served but to serve. God called them, as he does us, to minister to the real needs of others. That is the way Jesus used his power and authority and that is the way the disciples are to operate in the world.

But to insure that they understood, Jesus says, "Gentiles lord it over others; it shall not be so with you." Some would see in this statement an admonition against the use of power and authority. Quite the contrary! For if no one is empowered there is little progress, if no one is given authority there is no accountability. Even the most egalitarian societies, if they are to remain viable must have dynamic leadership incarnated in individuals. The Hebrew nation found that out. Initially established as a theocracy, they soon discovered that, due to human weakness, it was unable to cope with the problems it faced and so asked God's benediction on a monarchy. In our weakest moments a community of equals appeals to us because of our own insecurities and belligerence (we don't want anyone telling us what to do) and so we are apt to sacrifice the common good for our own ego needs and accompany it with all kinds of pious chatter.

Power in itself is not an evil thing, nor is the pursuit of it incompatible with God's design. The passion to learn, the pursuit of excellence — evidence of our desire for power — have been implanted in us as part of the Divine image. Indeed, Jesus promised power to the apostles (Acts 1:8) before he ascended. What is at issue here is not power as such but its use. Jesus saw power as an instrument not of control but of caring, as a vehicle not of submission but of servanthood.

Consider Jesus in relationship to those who surrounded him that night in the upper room. Some smugly folded their hands, pondering positions of power. Others firmly clenched their hands refusing to move, lest they reveal any sign of weakness. But Jesus reached out for the basin and the towel to serve the disciples even though he knew that they would betray and desert him that very night, and that he would be brought to trial and finally die by crucifixion. While the disciples were thinking only of themselves, Jesus, in whom the power of God resided, emptied himself and gave himself to those for whom he cared. He didn't worry about himself, how he felt, whom he could impress; the hands of the servant do not ask, "What will others think?" He saw the need, he rolled up his sleeves, he grabbed the basin and the towel and he went to work. In this humble but powerful way, Jesus began to transform the thinking of his disciples.

But like the disciples, it is hard for us to understand because we tend to use power as a show of force, to manipulate, to get what we want. It has always been that way. Go as far back in history as you wish, and you will see the problem illustrated. You will discover the struggle between the two approaches to the use of power, between the manipulator and the servant.

One can see the conflict in the Egyptian court when Moses the servant stood before Pharaoh the manipulator and cried, "Let my people go!" One can see it in the Roman court when Pilate, representing the kingdom of submission and domination, shouted, "Do you not know I have the power to free you or crucify you?" The polarities of power have always existed — that of manipulation and that of caring, that of submission and that of servanthood. Not so strange then that the disciples were taken aback by the Master who became the servant.

Following the pharaohs and the pilates has always been a temptation not only for people, but for nations and for churches. Often we feel powerless, so when we become part of a group which has clout, the temptation to exercise power like a sledgehammer is supremely seductive. And our generation has greater and more kinds of power at our disposal than any other peoples in all of history. We as a nation have more opportunities to serve this world in bringing peace and security than ever before, but we must constantly fight the urges of self-interest which, lording it over others, would alienate them from us.

The church is subject to the same uses of power. Basically there are two options. The first is to divide up into interest groups and bring the church to its knees, demanding that it submit to our ideas, utilize our language, conform to our concepts of what we want the church to do. The second is to selflessly serve in such a manner that we communicate the grace of God which can bring us together in ways which will make us truly great and strong.

Expecting Christians to be selflessness may be very idealistic because the trend in our society and in our church is not to turn outward but inward. Someone said, "You can tell the way society is heading by looking at the titles of our magazines. We used to have *Life*, then came *People*, and then *Us*. The next step, as we become increasingly self-centered, is Me." It should not have surprised me therefore to see on a newsstand the other day the magazine, *Self*.

Still God calls each of us to follow the example of Jesus by expending our lives in servanthood and service. That was clearly the message as Jesus instituted the sacrament of holy communion. In giving the bread and wine Jesus said to the disciples, "I am giving myself to you." From that moment on, when they received the Lord's supper they were reminded that they had also been called upon to give of themselves.

Today, too, the living Lord approaches us as we come to the altar and says, "Here, take and eat, this is my body. Take this cup and divide it among yourselves." Don't you see? Jesus asks us to keep doing this so that we might never forget that the servant Lord continues to give and give and give. One might say that the eucharist is "living proof" of God's expensive expenditure, that he did not count the cost but gave us everything he had to give. In this dynamic experience we become recipients of God's power and grace.

In the sacrament of the altar we view again the portrait painted by the Lord centuries ago in the upper room. Like the disciples before us we watch as Jesus gives unstintingly of himself, without thought as to what it cost him. Fatigue and personal pains are disregarded as Jesus stoops to serve. He does not share with us only superficial stuff. What he gives is not the leftovers of his life or the time he has to spare. He gives from the depths of his being, of his sweat, of his strength, and ultimately of his own body and blood.

So the scene drawn by Jesus that night in the upper room was one of a powerful servant motivated by an unrelenting love. In that moment the disciples were given an illustration of such impact that it would remain in memory as long as they had breath. His actions were those of an unabashed lover — giving a new dimension to the disciples' understanding of his life, his ministry. He loved without embarrassment, without reservation. He loved without requiring love in return. In spite of the stubborn pride of the disciples, Jesus went to work. And he says to us, as he said long ago to the disciples, "Do you know what I have done? I have given you an example that you also should do as I have done to you, so that as I was sent to serve, so send I you." He couldn't be clearer.

But we aren't to go off on our own without being empowered. So we have come to be fed with food for our faith, potent food, servant food. It isn't much, a little bit of bread and a swallow of wine, but when blessed by the Spirit it is enough, enough to nourish us for the life of powerful servanthood. Amen.

---

1. Wangerin, Jr., Walter. "Reliving the Passion," *Creative Communications for the Parish,* St. Louis, MO. p. 11

Good Friday
John 19:16b-22

The King Who Came To Die

"The King of the Jews." That was the title which Pilate nailed above the cross where Jesus hung. You would have thought the Jewish priests would have been glad to see this so-called king humiliated so. But no, it must be changed, "Do not write, 'The King of the Jews,' " they said, "but, write, 'This man said, I am King of the Jews.' " Without hesitating Pilate answered, "What I have written, I have written."

Perhaps Pilate's mind still burned with the memory of his encounter with the strange man whom he had sentenced to death a few hours earlier. It had been a disturbing experience.

The political-religious situation in Palestine was tense. It was the time of Passover and Rome wanted it to be observed peacefully. Now the priests had handed over to him a traveling preacher who was poor, but popular with the people. Jesus of Nazareth was ushered in to the praetorium. Pilate squinted through the early morning mist at the rumored rabble-rouser. With an air of superiority he leaned forward, glared at Jesus and began the interrogation, "Are you the King of the Jews?"

Jesus responded with a question of his own, "Do you say this of your own accord, or did others say it to you about me?"

In disgust Pilate said, "Who do you think I am? Your own people turned you over to me; what have you done?"

Then Jesus began to reveal who he was, "Don't worry, Pilate, my kingship is not of this world; if my kingship were of this world my servants would fight, that I might not be handed over to the Jews; but my kingship is not of this world."

Pilate pounced, "Ah! So you are a king?"

Jesus replied, "You say that I am a king. For this I was born, and for this I have come into the world, to bear witness to the truth."

On this Good Friday we come face to face with the mysterious sovereignty of our Lord and the nature of his strange kingdom. Pilate had a hard time understanding, and we do, too. Like Pilate we tend to think of kingdoms in terms of occupying land and controlling people.

Dr. Alvin Rogness, president emeritus of Luther-Northwestern Seminary suggests in his book, *Who Shall Be God,* that if such were the nature of God's rule then he could have come on a gigantic satellite which continually circled the globe and from which he could have keep an eye on every individual. His army, thousands upon thousands of angels, would be dispatched from his celestial throne to enforce his laws, punish disobedience and force people into bowing down before the Lord God. And we would live in fear and trembling of that dreadful God of the skies who could rain down terror and destruction at any moment and at any whim. Our lives would consist of tiptoeing anxiously through life lest we offend God in any way. We would have to be constantly on guard against his angelic army of avengers. If Christ's kingdom were of this world, he could make us knuckle under, but our hearts would remain unbent; he could earn our fear, but not our love. He could gain our obedience, but not our wills. Thank God Christ's kingdom is not patterned after earthly empires!

From the very beginning of the Old Testament, God began to sketch out the blueprint of his kingdom. It was boundless, there was room for everyone, and humankind was given the freedom to become a part of this glorious realm simply by developing a friendship with God which would develop into a relationship so close that eventually we, like Jesus, would even call the Almighty God, "Daddy (Mark 14:36)." It was a wonderful kingdom — the rules were few and the privileges many. It began with God, Adam and Eve. At first there was harmony of wills, respect, affection and concern for each other. That blueprint of God's kingdom has not changed.

But something went wrong. God's beautiful plan did not materialize. The world as we know it does not live in harmony with God. So what happened? The Old Testament tells us that it didn't take long for the man and woman to discover that the Lord God wasn't the only one vying for their loyalty. There were many other pretenders to the throne, would-be rulers who claimed their allegiance. While God was open and laid everything on the line, Satan teased, and taunted, and tempted Adam and Eve, subtly appealing to their self-glory, promising great things — pleasure, prosperity, even the prospect of being like gods themselves! They were duped, choosing to believe the lie rather than the truth. So the first couple rebelled against the benevolent kingdom of God and sin entered the world. The rest is history!

But Eve and Adam had no corner on gullibility. We know firsthand how seductive the voices which call out to us to follow them can be. The world presents us with an abundance of gods, a heady variety from which to choose the one or ones we will worship and serve. What began as one person's individual protest against God snowballed into a rebellion of such monstrous proportions that soon there was a question if God still had a kingdom. Humankind has not lost its resolve to challenge God's authority and the Lordship of Jesus the Christ.

The mighty God went on the offensive, sending leader after leader and prophet after prophet to the Hebrew people. This is the cycle their history followed. The people of Israel would get into trouble and appeal to God for help. God would send a great leader. At first the people would respond to God's servant; they would repent and return to the Lord God. Soon the nation would become strong and things would go smoothly again, and the people began to think they could get along without God. Then a foreign power would come and conquer them and they would cry to God for help. God would send a deliverer to help them and restore their nation. The people would become lax and turn from worshiping God. Over and over that scenario was played out.

Finally God permitted Israel to be swallowed up by their enemies. The nation of Judah was scattered abroad. Although a remnant of people remained faithful, the influence of God's kingdom was in doubt. Finally God decided to take matters into his own hands. He would come himself in human flesh; he would be the Light of the World and he would beat the devil at his own game!

So Jesus came, announcing that the kingdom of God had come in his appearing. "The kingdom of God is in the midst of you. It's right here," he would tell them, "just as I am standing among you." Appearances to the contrary, the rule of God came in force in the humble carpenter-teacher from Nazareth.

That was shocking news to the people of that day. They had been led to believe that when God's King, the Messiah came, he would usher in a realm of peace and prosperity and Israel would become a glorious political power once more. Indeed, the golden reign of King David was only a shadow of the glory which the Messiah would usher in when he began his reign in Jerusalem.

So Jesus' announcement that with his coming the kingdom of God had entered into their historical situation ran counter to their understanding of God's promise. They need only look around them to see that they were not surrounded by prosperity, but misery; they were not politically free but in bondage to the Romans. Who wants a God who does not bring economic, physical, and political advantages to his subjects?

That idea is still very much alive in another dress. The implication is that if you behave yourself and give your life to Christ, God will protect you from the "slings and arrows of outrageous fortune." It is a dangerous heresy. None of the saints in the New Testament experienced that kind of divine protection. What they found instead was a life fraught with danger and tribulation. They were satisfied with the security they found in knowing that Christ was with them; theirs was a peace in the midst of persecution. That is why Jesus said his kingship was not of this world, and that his peace was "not as the world gives (John 15:27)," for the world does not understand that as peace.

But it was still true: the kingdom of God was present in the midst of the misery, pain and bondage because Jesus was there. God came down from his palatial paradise to be with those who were burdened with poverty of body and soul. He squandered his heart on those who rebelled against him. He was no Messiah in pauper's clothing, privilege in disguise. Jesus lived out the truth that the kingdom of God was present in their pain, in their suffering, in their grief and in their guilt. No, his peace was not as the world perceives it, neither was his kingdom fashioned after earthly realms.

Now the drama quickly rises to its climax. Since God "emptied himself, taking the form of a slave, being born in human likeness (Philippians 2:7)," Jesus became, by all human standards, the foolishness of God, the weakness of God. Our Lord did not, like the Roman gods only appear to be human; he was not a hologram. Jesus was a mortal in every way; he was God made so vulnerable that he could suffer and die!

From the outset Jesus appears to be in over his head; he had given up his supernatural powers and then was forced to face the unbridled fury of the Prince of Darkness and all the mighty powers of this world. Satan, still stinging from his defeat at Jesus' hands in the wilderness, must certainly have been gloating. The tide had turned and his own people demanded his death — death — the most awesome weapon the evil one could use. The contest would soon be over and its outcome would have colossal implications — the kingship of the world was up for grabs!

So they took our Lord, and the henchmen of hate did their worst: humiliation, lashings, ridicule and public condemnation. Hear the spineless, craven Pilate say, " 'Shall I crucify your king?' The chief priests answered, 'We have no king but Caesar.' Then he handed him over to them to be crucified (John 19:15-16)." So they took the deposed king and led him to Golgotha, the place of the skull, a garbage dump where lives were discarded without the usual funeral formalities. And there he hung, our Lord, suspended between heaven and earth as though unacceptable to either. Hung there naked as a peeled grape! Some king. Some king.

Then he died. God died! The elements of the universe cried out with the anguish of an angry impossibility. How Satan must have rubbed his hands in glee. He did not know, could not know that at the very moment when he thought victory was at hand, God was ready to speak his word, a crushing word against which the devil could not stand. In Jesus' words, "It is accomplished!" the ingenious plan of God was finally revealed. With magnificent power he smashed right through death to life on the other side! He had beaten the devil on his own battlefield.

That means that the Messiah was King, not only of the living, but of all who have ever lived. His plan had never been to avoid the experience of death, to exempt himself from it. If Jesus was to be our Savior, sharing our humanity, then he also had to be subject to death. As the Bible says, in dying, Jesus "destroyed the one who has the power of death, that is, the devil, and freed those who all their lives had been held in slavery by fear of death (Hebrews 2:14b-15)".

So we gather this day, this Good Friday because one day the King of kings came to die that he might offer us life now, and for all eternity. That is why we call it Good Friday. Amen.

Easter Sunday
John 20:1-18

Good News From A Graveyard

If wild applause was ever in order in the church, Easter is the time. It is a day for Christians to cheerfully celebrate Christ's victory over death. Clearly the dominant mood in our worship this morning is joy. It is a day for breaking out the band, clapping hands and singing, "Hallelujah!"

But if you ever read the gospel accounts of the resurrection, you discover an unusual thing; the first reaction of the men and women who came to the tomb was not joy — it was bewilderment and fear! The immediately impact of the resurrection on the followers of Jesus was confusion and apprehension. Mary Magdalene was in shock and the disciples, regardless of John's comment that one of the disciples believed, were clearly unnerved by it all. After all, they went from that tomb and locked themselves in a secret room.

So it all adds up to this: Whatever else the followers of Jesus might have foreseen following the crucifixion, whatever they dreamed of, they did not anticipate a resurrection. That apparently was about the last thing they expected. The discovery of an empty tomb left them disconcerted, hesitant and scared.

If we are going to understand the power that is embedded in the very heart of Easter, we need to come to terms with the disciples' strange reaction of bewilderment and fear. That is hard to do because Easter comes as no surprise to us. We've been waiting for it all during Lent. We expect it. We plan for it.

For example, we already know the day on which Easter is going to be celebrated next year and perhaps even know where we are going to be. And because we expect it, we tend to lose the sense of amazement and surprise.

But while Easter's revelation of resurrection is anticipated by us, it took the disciples completely by surprise. A person who has been dead for three days doesn't just get up and begin living again; that would violate all the accepted laws of nature. They were intelligent people; they knew that.

So when Mary Magdalene, Peter and John encountered the risen Jesus, they didn't go walking off, hand in hand, into the sunset singing, "In the sweet by and by." Far from it! They were terrified. And we will need to come to an understanding of why they were afraid if we are going to plumb the depths of the resurrection and recapture the Easter ecstasy.

For one thing, if Jesus had really come back to life it would mean that they could never get away from God, even in death. That thought is more than a little frightening for it means that one's life is always subject to God's judgment; there is no forgetting; no escape.

If a person wanted to evade God, if they wanted to declare their independence from God, one of the first things they would need to do is eliminate the whole idea of resurrection. Indeed, our difficulties in believing the resurrection may be rooted in our desire to have the last word ourselves. For if death is the end, if there is nothing more, than through my dying, I speak the last word, not God. Then when I die, I will stay dead and that's that!

I wonder how many of us would like to believe that. It effectively takes care of the knotty problem of God. But it is motivated by the desire of the creature who insists that their bodies are their own to do with as they wish and that life's destiny lies, not in God's hands, but their own. Our basic instincts resist granting God power over our live or our death!

Furthermore belief in the resurrection means that we are exposed to the shocking way sin which God purposes to work in this world. It seems the Lord God is rather careless about the means by which the Divine will is done, using anything that is at hand: mangers, leper colonies, crosses and graves. There is nothing sanitary or clinical about the way God's grace works in the world. That makes one wonder what God is up to, what is coming next.

The followers of Jesus were confused and disheartened by his death. They wept at the cross. They wept at the tomb. But they accepted it. We read that the women came early, while it was still dark, presumably to anoint Jesus' body with embalming spices. They had accepted the fact that he was dead. They resigned themselves to that; after all, we eventually all die. They were ready to pick up their lives where they had dropped them when he died.

Many of you here today have learned to come to terms with grief. You have come to accept the grim reality of death. We learn to carry on. We have to. But part of the great astonishment for those initial followers was the realization that God works through suffering and death. The terrible tragedy which took place on Calvary was all part of God's plan!

I'm sure that those first disciples believed that there was an abundant life in the hereafter; Jesus had talked about it often enough. But they did not consider the possibility that God's lofty purposes of grace would be accomplished through things like suffering and death. It is one thing to deal with the harsh realities like death and disillusionment, to live with them, to accept them — but it is another thing entirely to face the reality that this is often the way God chooses to work in this world. These are the methods by which God's purposes are carried out. Now they knew. God does not save us from suffering and death. God saves us through them. This fallen, sinful world was brought back into the loving embrace of God through the sufferings and death of Jesus, God's own Son.

We wonder, "What does this mean?" Then we recall that when we were baptized, the imprint of the cross was made on us as a sign that we would not only share in the power of Jesus' resurrection, but that we would know the fellowship of his sufferings. Thus the promise of God is that society's ills will be cured and world recreated, so that it recovers its lost beauty, its lost meaning, through the suffering of Christians in this world. God's people are called to share the sufferings of Christ.

In its milder forms it might mean we are called to give up the status symbols others think are so important or we might take seriously the whole matter of ecology. On a deeper level we might be required to take unpopular stands that will result in lost friends or alienated family.

There is another aspect to the bewilderment and fear of Jesus' followers which we must not overlook in our pursuit of the meaning of the resurrection. Before those first men and women could experience giddy glory of Easter, they had to come to terms with the fact that with Jesus' resurrection came judgment. For when they buried Jesus in the sepulcher, they buried some other things with him. They buried their hopes and dreams for a Messianic kingdom. They buried all the love and care Jesus had poured out uponthe world, especially for the unlovely and the life-worn, the bruised ones. All that was entombed with him.

But that was not all. They also buried a lot of other things, things best forgotten. They buried their self-centered quarrels about who was the greatest. They buried their petty jealousies and the ugly, sordid scenes of denial and betrayal. All that had been interred with him, and good riddance! Paul Tillich says that Jesus' burial was a powerful symbol which suggested to the disciples that all things could now be put behind them. Buried was the fact that they had all, in cowardice, forsaken him and fled. It was reasonable now for them to assume that they could pick up the pieces of their lives, their shattered aspirations and somehow get on with life.

Then, as the news of Jesus' resurrection is relayed from one incredulous follower to another, another emotion engulfs them — fear! They are afraid because now what they thought had died has come to life again, it all comes back. They must meet, face to face, the one whom they have betrayed, blasphemed and forsaken. Apparently there is no forgetting. No wonder the disciples were afraid. Instead of being able to forget, they would be forced to relive their shame!

Perhaps that is why the gospel accounts often speak as the first word not, "be of good cheer." But rather, "Do not be afraid." Do not be afraid. For the one who brings everything back to life again is the One who loves you and gave himself for you. The one who permits no escape, no forgetting, even in death, is the one who remembers and loves you still. Oh yes, he is a reckless lover. Of course no one deserves that love, the first followers didn't and we don't either; that is not the point. The point is God and the Easter exclamation that God loves you. Thank God there is no escape from that love. No escape, even in death!

That was Mary Magdalene's experience. Her encounter with Jesus made it clear. When he spoke, such love and acceptance emanated from his words that in joy she ran to him pell-mell so she might be embraced by him. He had sought her out in love and compassion; he came to the disciples in the same way . . . and he still comes to you and you and to me, lovingly, compassionately.

That ought to mean a great deal to us for it means we don't have to run from God any more. We don't have to try to hide. We don't have to pretend, to God, or to others, or to ourselves. It means that Jesus comes back, not in condemnation, not in judgment, but in grace and peace. Do you understand that? Our Lord comes back to resurrect us so that we who are dead in our sins and don't have to live in guilt any more, we don't have to be afraid of God or judgment.

Easter proclaims that all the doors that shut us in — fear, guilt, anxiety, insecurity — they are all overcome and the doors are now opened. Christ offers to open those doors and give you your freedom. He opens the last door to us, too, the door of death. You might say, "When I die I will stay dead," but that is not true. You didn't ask to be born, but you were born. You didn't choose to be born, but you were. You didn't decide to wake up this morning, but you did. Perhaps it was because somebody called you and you awoke. So you will not be asked to be raised from the dead, but you will be. For Christ will call you and you will arise and he will give you life. If that is what you want, that is the way it will be.

How strange that it all came out of a grave. But then that is rather like God. Out from the Nuremberg war trials in post-World War II Germany, comes the witness of one man. During the war near Willma, Poland, a group of Jews who had escaped death in the gas chambers took refuge in a cemetery. They lived there, huddled and hidden in the bottom of dug graves. A baby boy was born one evening in one of those graves. The grave-digger, an old, strict, orthodox Jew, clothed in a linen shroud, assisted in the birth. When that newborn uttered its first cry, the old grave-digger exclaimed, "Great God, have you finally sent the Messiah to us? For who else than the Messiah would be born in a grave?"

Born in a grave. That's us, you know. Our lives literally came out of a grave! How like God to do something like that. Born in a grave. Born to celebrate. Born to leap for joy, to live in anticipation because God's resurrecting power has been let loose in this world.

That is the good news from the graveyard: Jesus Christ is risen from the dead so that you and I might live in the assurance that all the doors of life and death are now opened to us. That is the conquest of the cross, the victory of Easter. This triumphant message is illustrated powerfully in a scene from T.S. Eliot's *Murder In the Cathedral.*

A number of priests are working to bar the doors to the church. They are barring the doors against men who seek to assassinate the Archbishop of Canterbury. Thomas, the Archbishop, will not permit it even though he knows it is for his own safety. He says to the priests, "Unbar the door. Throw upen the doors! I will not have the house of prayer, the church of Christ, the sanctuary turned into a fortress. The church shall be open, even to our enemies, open the door!"

The priests think he's gone mad; they protest. They tell him that he would bar the door against wild animals, why not against men who have become like beasts?

His answer rings out clearly, "We have fought the beasts and have conquered. Now is the triumph of the cross. Open the door. I command it! Open the door!"

So we are invited to open the door and step out into life with the wonder of the Easter message: that Christ not only lives, he is life-giving, life transforming, life-resurrecting.

How terribly frustrating it is to convey this awesome truth. For I feel and believe more about othis good news than I can say. Its truth is overwhelming, far outrunning our capacity to express or understand. I encourage you simply to take and run with it. Or better yet, let it possess you. I invite you to go out from this place, asking God to live out your life with the kind of abandoned joy and righteousness which is fitting for one who has received so very much. God bless you Easter and the celebration of its marvelous power in your life. Amen.

Easter 2
John 20:19-31

A Word For All Reasons

Easter has happened. Jesus, crucified on Friday is risen from the dead, and from that time-shattering event he sets out. To do what? What shall be the first item on his agenda? We don't know what our Lord did between the early morning appearance to Mary Magdalene and the evening, but we do know that revealing himself to the disciples was high on his list of priorities. One question which could be asked is this one: Knowing what we do about Jesus' arrest, trial, sentencing, and the behavior of his followers, including people like Judas and Peter, what would you expect that Jesus would say to them? And a similar question: Aware of the way in which the disciples abandoned their Lord, what do you suppose they expected to hear?

In our imagination, let us transport ourselves to Jerusalem on the evening of the day of resurrection. Ten of the 11 disciples move nervously about in the too small room. Their palms are wet with the sweat of anxiety and they are caught up in a violent storm of emotions. The death of Jesus had been a cruel blow. Not only did they lose the loving presence of the One who was above all an understanding friend, but they were leaderless as well. With Jesus' humiliating defeat, all they had lived for and hoped for had crumbled beneath them. There in the dust lay their ruined goals, the ridiculous remains of their grand dreams. Oh, they had heard the rumors rumbling through the city streets, the story of some women that Jesus had risen from the dead, but "it seemed to them an idle tale." A couple of the disciples had verified that the tomb was empty, but that only unnerved them all the more. As remote as a resurrection would be, if Jesus had risen he would have certainly have contacted them by now. As it was, there was no evidence of Jesus' body, dead or alive.

To make matters worse, there were stories being spread throughout the land that the Jewish leaders had ordered the arrest and death of all the disciples, in order that this religious menace might be put to an end, once and for all. So each man in turn, as he paces the floor, mindlessly checks the lock on the door and the latches of the windows, just to be sure they are secure.

It is an eerie atmosphere; no one speaks. Each is imprisoned in his private thoughts; each involved in an inner war. One part of them prays that the rumors are true, that the resurrection of Jesus is not just wishful thinking, that somehow he has survived the ordeal. Another part of them is filled with the fear that he might be risen. Fear, because they did not look forward to meeting him. Indeed, would they dare to look him in the eyes again after they had failed him so miserably? What would he say? What would he do? They had shamefully abandoned him. Would he return to them or would he go out to find other disciples, disciples who would believe in him, who would stand by him? They were filled with self-reproach and despair hung heavy about them. What thoughts must have tormented them at that dreadful time?

Suddenly, without announcement, without fanfare, silently, forcefully, Jesus appears in the middle of the room, in spite of the locked doors. He utters four words, "Peace be with you." Peace be with you. No words could have meant more to those disciples, no words packed with more power for healing, and wholeness. There were many reasons for the despondency and anxiety of the disciples, numerous reasons why they stood paralyzed in that moment. But Jesus' invocation of peace was a word for all their reasons. Those four words went to the heart of the matter and ministered to their insecurity and loneliness, their overwhelming guilt, their sense of despair and the great fears which had immobilized them.

Consider that the disciples had good cause to be frightened on that Easter evening. At that point in time they were not sure of many things, but they were absolutely convinced of one thing: Jesus had died. At least he had been dead. Then, as out of a whirlwind, a figure appears and immediately their sense of security is blown away and they realize how very vulnerable they are. Who is this specter and what does he want from them? Already they feared for their lives at the hands of the Hebrew soldiers and now this. That the disciples quaked with fear is a gross understatement. To that fear, that trepidation, Jesus spoke his word of peace. It wasn't just the fact that he spoke it, I believe it was the way in which he said it that brought life back into the spirits of those disciples.

That powerful word of Christ spoke also to the enormous burden of guilt they bore. They had not only deserted their Lord and Master, but had denied him, failed him. Not only had their faith proved inept and powerless and their resources of courage been woefully inadequate, but they had shown themselves to be utterly shameless. Consider. If it had not been for Joseph of Arimathea, what would have happened to the body of the crucified Christ? Like the bodies of all criminals it would have been ruthlessly torn from the cross and carelessly thrown on the garbage dump, fair prey for the creatures of carrion. By nightfall, birds would have pecked out his eyes and the scavenger animals would have torn all the flesh from his bones. The thought is grotesque and repulsive. But that is what made the disciples' cowardice and inaction so scandalous, and their guilt so overwhelming. They had, in faithless fear, abandoned the Lord's body to be mutilated, desecrated. All this Jesus takes into account when he utters those incredible words of grace and forgiveness, "Peace be with you." It was for good reason that the disciples felt guilty and only Jesus' word of peace could bring forgiveness and restoration.

It's a small wonder that the Bible says, "Then the disciples were glad when they saw the Lord." Glad? I'll bet they were ecstatic! What incredible power was at work here. Out of mourning there blossomed rejoicing. Where once ambitions and visions lay crushed, now exciting new possibilities had been born. Out of fear and depression sprang happiness and hope, creating at atmosphere of glory and joy. Guilt and remorse were forgotten in forgiveness and the disciples reveled in the warmth of reconciliation. With a simple word from Jesus' lips, stomachs which had been turned inside out were calmed, and minds which were raw with remorse were soothed. It happened because Jesus did not come with angry words of judgment or criticism, or disappointment (although the situation would certainly have warranted it). Indeed, there were many reasons why this initial meeting of Jesus and his disciples could have been disastrous, many reasons why they could have walked away demoralized and beaten. But Jesus came with a word of peace. A word for all reasons.

It's amazing isn't it, how, with a remarkable economy of words, Jesus was able to transfigure the situation and put his rag-tag corps of apostles back on the track again? The reconciliation had been successful and Jesus' peace began to take control, except for Thomas who had missed Jesus' dramatic, post-resurrection appearance.

When the other disciples finally located him, they tried to convince him that Jesus had risen and had met their pain with his balm of peace. Why Thomas had such difficulty in believing is not hard to understand. Crucified and buried people just don't get up and start living again. The other disciples may have been suckered in by some clever deception, but not Thomas. Oh no! He was a realist. And furthermore, if Jesus had returned, his words certainly would not have been kind, not after the way they had behaved. They deserved judgment and Thomas knew it. Perhaps that is one reason why he remained unconvinced in spite of the united testimony of the other apostles.

In any case Thomas also suffered from fear and a sense of failure. He knew the same guilt and shame which had plagued the other disciples, and his rejection of the so called "resurrection" only added to his anguish. His friends seemed to be living in a state of denial, refusing to accept the fact that Jesus was dead, that he no longer would be with them. But he was still tormented by it.

Something, however, stirred within Thomas. Previously he had been content to be off by himself. Since the day of the apparition of Jesus, however, the disciples seemed to be dramatically changed and Thomas sought their company more and more. Then one day, when Thomas was with the disciples, Jesus once again appeared in the room without warning. There was a moment of shocked silence as the Lord turned, his eyes locked on those of Thomas. The "doubting disciple" must have cowered beneath Christ's piercing gaze, yet there radiated no condemnation but compassion, not judgment, but love. Then Jesus spoke the words, "Peace be with you." There is no doubt that they are aimed directly at Thomas. These four words reached out to embrace him with an absolutely awesome affection. At that moment he experienced the wonder of forgiveness, just as the other disciples had eight days earlier. All the shortcomings, the sins and the failures of Thomas put together were incapable of stemming the flood of God's grace. All of the reasons why Jesus should reject him and condemn him came tumbling down. Even his persistent doubt was not held against him. His faithlessness was more than conquered by Christ's word of peace. Though he was faithless God remained faithful for God cannot deny himself (2 Timothy 2:13). So it was true for Thomas as well, that Christ's word of peace was a word for all reasons.

That is the good news. Jesus still comes with his word of grace. He still comes to woo us, to forgive us, to enthrall us with his love. No matter how many reasons we may have for holding him at arm's length, for shutting him out of our lives, they are as nothing when he speaks his words for all reasons, "Peace be with you." Those potent, piercing words slice through all our pretenses, surmount all our weaknesses, forgive all our sinfulness, abolish all our guilt, and overcome all our fears and our faithlessness. Not even our worst doubts can keep him from claiming our hearts. And he will not stop speaking his word until it can be said of us, as it was said of the disciples, "They were glad when they saw the Lord."

"Peace be with you." That is God's word, that is our Lord's gift to you this morning, as you face this week, as you struggle with your daily problems and cope with the endless routines of everyday life. They are words which briefly but eloquently capture and express the hope of Easter, that God is alive, that our Lord is with you, that the Spirit comes to bless you with this incredible, all-purpose word of grace. So great and vivid is it, that it radiates an atmosphere of Easter upon all your days; all your days and weeks and years. Even at the moment of your death, even then, that message will be sufficient, as it is spoken by someone who shares with you the word of the Lord, a word for all reasons, "Peace be with you." Amen.

Easter 3
John 21:1-14

Act III, Scene 2

Each year we in the church are involved in a great drama. Although the script is ancient, thousands of years old, its message is as new as today and as hopeful as tomorrow. It has been played out on countless stages throughout the world, and the story is so incredible that in spite of its constant retelling, it never grows stale, is never irrelevant. It is always fresh, always worth hearing and it always brings healing and strength.

Act I, Scene 1 of this churchwide drama began with the season of Advent as we prepared for our Lord's coming. The glorious climax of the first Scene was Christmas, the enchanting birth of the Christ-child. The second Scene of Act 1 is called "the season of Epiphany." It opened with the visitation of the wisemen and every event thereafter proceeded to reveal Jesus as the Son of God, portraying his startling ministry in our midst.

Act II followed. Its title was Lent, or the Season of Sorrows. We observed Jesus as he faced the difficult decisions which led him to Jerusalem. At Gethsemane we saw him in agony as he prayed, "Father, if it be thy will, let this cup pass from me; nevertheless, not my will, but thine be done." We looked on as he was arrested, ridiculed and condemned. We witnessed the darkness descending over the world as our Lord was crucified, and we felt the fury of nature when he died. Then we saw him lowered from the cross and laid in a tomb. The long and powerful Act II ended with our Lord dead, the disciples guilt-ridden and grief-stricken, and all of Jerusalem in an uproar over the events which had taken place.

Act III, Scene 1 created a totally different mood. Its brief first scene took us to an empty tomb where we learned the surprise announcement, "He is not here . . . He has risen!" We listened to the shouts of joy which exploded from the mouths of Jesus' followers and echoed down the streets of Jerusalem and out into the world. We saw that some doubted, but then Jesus dropped in to see his friends; he let them touch him, and he reached out to them with a blessing of peace. The Scene closed with Jesus preparing his disciples for their ministry in the world.

At this point it is natural to feel that the drama is over, that we ought to get up from our seats, so to speak, and prepare to leave the theater. It appears that all of the significant things have happened. The Jesus story appears to have ended somewhat "happily ever after," so why stick around for the credits?

But wait a moment, Act III isn't over . . . not yet. There's another scene to come! While Act III, Scene 2 is not a fireworks festival in the church it is an essential part of Jesus' ministry on Earth. As the curtain rises, we see Jesus doing a very unusual thing. Following his upper room appearance to the disciples after the resurrection, he spends the next 40 days mysteriously gliding in and out of their lives. For almost six weeks he suddenly appears before them, and then just as quickly disappears. Forty days of occasional, brief, and apparently random encounters. Why? For what purpose?

It is hard to make sense of it. One post-resurrection appearance should have been all that was needed. Certainly a second manifestation would have convinced even the most skeptical of Christ's followers. After all, seeing a man who had been murdered, and buried in a tomb for three days, now very much alive, isn't something you would likely forget!

If Jesus had used those 40 days to travel around Palestine showing up in places like Herod's palace, or Pilate's praetorium, or the Temple of Caiaphas, that would have been reasonable. He could have shown those people who really had the power and the glory. Tempting as that might have been for you or me, he didn't do that. He kept contacting the same people, ever so briefly, over and over and over again for 40 days!

Jesus simply moved in and out of the lives of his friends. For example, as two men are walking on the road to Emmaus, Jesus catches up to them, and without being recognized, accompanies them. He hears them tell about the terrible events of the past few days, of the horrible fate of the young rabbi from Nazareth; how he was unjustly condemned and crucified. On hearing this Jesus doesn't rattle them by saying, "But look, I'm Jesus and I'm not dead! See, I'm very much alive." Rather, he lets them talk. As the day comes to an end, the two men invite Jesus to stay and share a meal, and only as he prays do they suddenly become aware that he is the Christ who was dead and buried. But it seems no sooner do they recognize him, than he vanishes.

Or consider the gospel for today. Some disciples go fishing. They fish all night, catching nothing. Then a man appears on the shore instructing them to cast the nets to the other side. Suddenly their nets are full of fish. It is then that the apostle John realizes that this is Jesus risen from the dead and he cries out, "It is the Lord!" Impulsively and with joy Peter jumps into the water and swims for shore. Soon the other disciples arrive, they join in breakfast and have a wonderful time together. But as abruptly as he came, he left.

Why? What reason can there be for such behavior? Let's look at these post-resurrection appearances. They have several things in common.

First, when Jesus intercepts the lives of his friends he always does so gracefully. That is, he doesn't disrupt their lives by making spectacular entrances or by half scaring the wits out of them. Rather, he flows in and out of their lives with remarkable ease, always showing love and compassion.

Secondly, he stays with his hosts for only as long as he senses they have a need for him. Then he disappears quietly. Indeed, these appearances became so natural that the apostles soon start taking them for granted. We know because the writer of the book of Acts states that Jesus continued to appear and disappear for 40 days, yet the biblical writers have recorded only the initial visitations; apparently they became so common that they were no longer newsworthy!

A third characteristic is that Jesus always let people discover for themselves who he was. In other words, he never forced himself on people, never made a big deal about his presence. So gentle and natural were his arrivals that his followers sometimes had to "concentrate" to be aware of his nearness.

In light of this evidence it seems Jesus was using the principle of repetition to impress on his disciples that he could move in and out of their lives, effortlessly at will. He was saying, "I am always near you. Always. I can come to you at a moment's notice. Indeed, I may appear before you at any time; in whatever situation you may find yourself, I am never far from you." For 40 days the disciples experienced the ever-possible presence of the Lord, so that even when he was not visible it felt as though he were there. They never knew for sure when he would appear, but they expected him at any time, knowing that in the twinkling of an eye, he could be there, standing with them.

With that lesson learned, the disciples were able to accept fearlessly the challenge of spreading the gospel in a hostile world. They faced the lion's hungry jaws and gladiators' fearful spears, with songs of praise to God because they knew Christ was with them. They knew it, knew he could appear at a moment's notice. They lived faithfully in the truth of Jesus' final words, "Lo, I am with you always." Those were not mere words of hope, they composed a promise, a promise which had been fortified by the experiences of 40 days. Act III, Scene 2, what a beautiful way Christ chose to impress on his followers that he was always near them.

As Act IV begins, we see that God's drama in the world has not come to an end. This long scene began as the Holy Spirit gripped the disciples and inspired them to give their lives for the glory of God and for the benefit of all Christians to follow. Act IV continues as the risen Christ still visits his people to be close to them, to minister to their needs, to support them in their struggles, to equip and strengthen them for Christian service. The work of Christ goes on and will go on until he comes again.

The good news for us is that Jesus' promise of presence was not meant only for his friends in the dim and dusty past. His promise was intended for all of his disciples in all times and places. It was meant also for you and me. True, he doesn't materialize in front of us, but we sense he is here. Inwardly we know he is near. We are not able to touch him, but he can and has touched us. True to form, Jesus comes to us just as he appeared so long ago to his friends. That is, he flows in and out of our lives so naturally that unless we take time for meditation and quietness, we may not even know that he has come.

That truth was experienced even by Elijah of Old Testament. He expected the Lord to make a big fuss when appearing to him at Mount Horeb. But the Bible says, "Now there was a great wind, so strong that it was splitting mountains and breaking rocks in pieces before the Lord, but the Lord was not in the wind; and after the wind an earthquake, but the Lord was not in the earthquake, and after the earth quake was a fire, but the Lord was not in the fire; and after the fire a sound of sheer silence (1 Kings 19:11b-12).'' The sheer silence, that was the Lord! The RSV translates God's presence as, "a still small voice." The point is, God doesn't overpower us but comes with quiet peace to captivate our hearts.

Most comforting is the knowledge that our Lord comes to us when we need him most. Even then he doesn't announce his presence, or shock us into recognition. He comes to us in quietness: in the hollows of grief; the soundless, emptiness of anxiety, the silent trembling of guilt. But he comes. He comes. The truth is, he may slip into your life at this very moment — or the next. You cannot predict his visitations. But your awareness can be sensitized by practicing the presence of God. You can live in the awareness of our Lord's nearness through faithful prayer and by envisioning him with you.

That discipline is poignantly illustrated in the oft told story of an old man who suddenly became gravely ill. When the pastor came for a visit he noticed a chair beside the bed. "Oh my goodness," he said, "You must have already had company today."

The old man said, "No, but let me tell you the story of the chair. Years ago I told a friend that when I prayed at night I frequently fell asleep right in the middle, or I just couldn't concentrate on what I was praying about. So this friend suggested that I put a chair by my bed and imagine that Jesus was sitting there because, you know, he's promised to be with us. So, I started doing that and, you know, it made a big difference. Sometimes I even think I see him sitting there."

After having communion with the man, the pastor left. Later that evening he got a call from the daughter. She said, "Dad just died. Can you come over?" So the pastor went to see her. The daughter said, "You know, I was in the room and dad seemed okay, he wasn't struggling or anything. I left for just a minute. When I came back, he had peacefully died. But there was something quite strange. Somehow, he had managed to turn over on his side and stretch out his arm and place his hand on the chair."

That's living in the presence of Christ. And it happens. It can happen for you, as it can happen for me, at any time. Oh, not to all in the same way, because Christ comes to each of us individually and uniquely. But in solitude and need he will come. He will come because he has promised! Amen.

Easter 4
John 10:22-30

Safe With The Shepherd

Listening to a television talk-show one night I heard the cartoonist Jules Pfeiffer discussing a comic strip he once drew. In it, a little boy was afraid to go to school because he thought his parents might move away while he was gone. He didn't want to go to bed at night becuse he feared that his parents might die while he slept. "Coping with fears is a terrific battle for a child," said Pfeiffer. "It's like being on 24-hour guard duty." He went on to say that he had received many letters about the cartoon from adults who said that it was that way for them, too, that you don't have to be a child to feel surrounded by fear.

Sometimes it feels like fear is lurking around a corner or hovering over our heads. It attacks us at different levels. Some fears are relatively minor. What is going to happen tomorrow? Will it rain on my parade? Will I get sick?

Other fears reach down into our entrails and twist our stomachs into knots: Do people like me? Will I make it through this crisis? What if things don't turn out the way I want? What is going to become of me at last?

With all the pressures we feel and all the possibilities for evil, is it any wonder that we live with increasing insecurity? If we are not worrying about ourselves, we are concerned for our families or our friends, or about pollution, or global war. There always seems to be something. It is like being on 24-hour guard duty and it doesn't make any difference how old you are.

The words of our gospel from the Apostle John were written to Christians who were also on "guard duty," suffering hardships and persecution. Not only did they have to deal with the customary distresses of life, but they faced questions such as, "Would they be arrested? And if so, how would they die?" Would they be whipped to death, forced to fight the gladiators, fed to the lions? Theirs were frightful issues of life and death. Let's look at how John reached out to minister to the temptations and insecurities of the people of his day by telling a story about Jesus.

He relates the Lord's parable of the Good Shepherd. "Jesus," says John, "is the Good Shepherd." He is the trustworthy one who is willing to lay down his life for his sheep-like people. Trust Jesus for he will shepherd you safely through life. And how do you know you are on the path? You follow the word of Jesus into the green pastures, for he says, "My sheep hear my voice; I know them, and they follow me."

The call of our Lord, however, is "hidden" in a whole chorus of worldly voices which beckon us. Other would-be shepherds seek to tempt us away from the Good Shepherd, the joy of his forgiveness and the security of his love. And when we are weak and confused we may fall victim to the enticements of other gods.

I am reminded of an American tourist who was traveling in the Mid East. He came upon several shepherds whose flocks had intermingled while drinking water from a brook. After an exchange of greetings, one of the shepherds turned toward the sheep and called out, "Manah. Manah. Manah." (Manah means "follow me" in Arabic.) Immediately his sheep separated themselves from the rest and followed him.

Then one of the two remaining shepherds called out, "Manah. Manah." and his sheep left the common flock to follow him. The traveler then said to the third shepherd, "I would like to try that. Let me put on your cloak and turban and see if I can get the rest of the sheep to follow me."

The shepherd smiled knowingly as the traveler wrapped himself in the cloak, put the turban on his head and called out, "Manah. Manah." The sheep did not respond to the stranger's voice. Not one of them moved toward him. "Will the sheep ever follow someone other than you?" The traveler asked.

"Oh yes," the shepherd replied, "sometimes a sheep gets sick, and then it will follow anyone."

We have seen it, haven't we? People, young and old, who are "sick." Battered by the storms of life and distracted by voices urging them to go this way and that, they have lost their bearings and they don't know where they are or where they are going. That can be more than a little frightening; it leads to despair, to hopelessness. And when someone is "sick" they will follow anyone who will promise a moment of happiness, a brief feeling of peace or forgetfulness, a sense that they are someone.

The call of Jesus the Good Shepherd is, "I am the Way, the Truth, and the Life." There is no better way, no greater truth, no happier life. Our Lord reaches out to us in love that we might follow him.

Sometimes in fear or desperation we chose to follow no one and instead turn inward and try to "lift ourselves up by our own bootstraps," as if that were possible. But the Way, the Truth and the Life cannot be discovered within one's self. That's why you can read all the self-help books in the world and still be lost, confused, and frightened. No self-oriented accomplishments — attaining power, amassing wealth, gaining status or receiving the applause of the crowd — will give enduring fulfillment, security of purpose, or abiding peace, no matter what the world says.

We have invested our time, money and faith in false gods. That is the reason for the anxiety, the sense of hopelessness, and turmoil of our world. That is why fear grips us. Don't you see? All the gods are dying! All the idols we have fashioned for ourselves, all the would-be shepherds we have followed, all the gods we have preferred before the Lord God have failed us. We followed them, only to watch them die. When the chips are down, when we are up against it, when we turn for help, we discover our gods have vanished. That can be terrifying! It can be terrifying to see the shepherds we have followed passing away, to see the gods we have loved and trusted and worshiped and pursued — materalism or pleasure, or popularity, or security, or whatever — to see them die because they are inadequate to speak to the deepest needs of our hearts and lives.

The trouble for many is that they have abandoned the church, or at least relegated it to a "bit role" in their life; it is a convenience at best. Thus the power of forgiveness, the gifts of grace, the warmth of fellowship are absent. When people no longer worship they lose sight of the beacons which warn us of the life-shattering rocks, they often forfeit the Word of God which lights the path. They find themselves in need of a Shepherd but they don't know where to look. Author Romain Gary describes it well in his book, *The Ski Bum.*

A Dominican priest speaks to a group of young people at a ski resort. He says, "You are all no more than 20 or 22 years old, but yours is an empty existence, I'm telling you. Nothing sings for you anymore. You're so angry with all the hypocrisy, all the phony piper's tunes, that you end up by breaking all the pipes and hating all the tunes. You reduce the world to a spiritual shambles. God is ha-ha-ha. The Soul is ho-ho-ho. Booze is your comfort. Love is reduced to sex. Family — what's that? Are you kidding? So now you are left with nothing. But before I go I shall say one more word."

"Oh God," says one of the skiers.

"Yes, yes," replies the priest, "That's right . . . Oh God. But the point is, you dumped him and life didn't become more enjoyable. Something is still missing isn't it? You got rid of God, and isn't that funny, something is still missing. Perhaps you ought to try to get rid of yourselves a little. Perhaps you will end up by getting rid of yourselves as well. I would begin with that if I were you. That's a riddle that comes from an American children's game. The question is, 'Who took the cookie from the cookie jar?' I see you know the game; very interesting. You are all very bright and clever so maybe you'll find an answer. Who took the cookie from the cookie jar, indeed? Shall we blame Freud or Marx? Or maybe it was prosperity, materialism, or hard-boiled realism. I don't know and I don't care. But you certainly seem to be missing the cookie very much. You twist and turn and ache looking for it."[1]

That's the future for those who follow some superficial shepherd down a primrose path littered with promises of pleasure and satisfaction. Ultimately he deserts us, dies on us, leaves us lost, bewildered, twisting and turning and aching. That is what is happening in our time. The gods are dying; they always do and that is a fearsome thing because we have staked our life on them.

So we hold before each other the option of following the Good Shepherd, to declare with our lips and our lives he is indeed the Way, the Truth and the Life. It is the Good Shepherd who beckons to us in our heartbreak and our loneliness, calls out to us in our guilt and in our dying. When we come to him he brings his love to our lovelessness and his power to our powerlessness so that now there is healing, now there is forgiveness, now there is direction to living, and life undying. That is the promise, "I give you life eternal and nothing in all creation will ever be able to snatch you out of my hand."

It is true that coping with our fears is a terrific battle; sometimes it seems overwhelming. We need all the help we can get. We need a Shepherd who will stand sentinel over our lives so that we can rest, knowing his mighty power will sustain us. No other god will do; we need the Good Shepherd who will lead us in the right Way, teach us the liberating Truth and give us strength for Life and peace and security at this life's end.

One of my favorite stories illustrates this for us in a poignant way. There was a little boy named Jimmy, who was the youngest of three children born into a wealthy Canadian family. He had been sickly since he was an infant, but in his fifth year his illness grew worse and he could no longer walk.

His parents spared no cost in seeing that Jimmy received the best medical care available. They purchased an electric wheelchair so that he could get around by himself, and any toy he wanted was his for the asking. As the months progressed it became obvious that Jimmy could not hang on much longer. The parents were anxious, wondering if they should say anything to him about his illness or if they should tell him he was dying. Although they belonged to no church, the father knew a man whom he respected and who was a Christian. He went to the man to ask his advice.

The man shared many things about life and death and about God's greatest gift of grace in Jesus. Then he said, "I like to teach young children this short Bible verse. Perhaps you could teach it to Jimmy. There's one word for each finger on the left hand: 'The Lord is my shepherd.' It's easy for them to learn, and afterward I explain the love of God in that verse. I always tell them," he said, "to hold on to the fourth finger, the Lord is my shepherd, because that means I belong to Jesus."

The father went home and taught Jimmy the Bible verse, doing his best to explain its meaning, and telling him to grasp the fourth finger on his left hand. Jimmy was delighted and repeated it many times a day.

One morning Jimmy's mother rushed in to get his father. "Jimmy's gone," she said, sobbing. "He's gone. But look. Look."

The father ran to his son's room and looked in. There was Jimmy, silent in death, but his hands were in front of his face, and his right hand was clasped tightly around the fourth finger of his left hand.

That father taught his son many things and gave him many possessions, but nothing he did for Jimmy was as valuable as introducing him to the Good Shepherd. The important thing for Jimmy was not that he had all the facts straight on Jesus, but that he was aware that Jesus, the Son of God, knew about him, and loved him. When you are weak and vulnerable it is good to know that someone so powerful comes to you personally, so that you might have the security and joy of knowing that, come what may, you will be cared for and provided for because you belong to Jesus.

Today I invite you to listen to the call of the Good Shepherd, to accept his invitation to let him be your God. He comes declaring his love and promising to be your God forever. Eternal power he offers through the Holy Spirit, and safe passage through the uncertainties of life. That is the good news I have for you today. You belong to Jesus. Follow him, for he is the Way of salvation. He is the Truth that endures forever.

He is the Life that does not end. Jesus will give you the security of knowing where you are going, what you believe, and what you will be at last. Jesus loves you and you are safe with the Shepherd. Amen.

---

1. Printed by permission. Gary, Romain. *The Ski Bum*. Bantam Books. Harper and Row Publishers, Inc. 1966. pp. 123-125.

Easter 5
John 13:31-35

A Strange Kind Of Glory

It is often difficult for Christians to get past the idea that those who have given themselves to the Lord should be treated a little better than the average woman or man who does not possess a living faith. In other words, there ought to be some kind of return for what you have done for God, for what you have given in time, energy and money. That doesn't sound outrageous, does it? In this "you get what you deserve" world, you really ought to be rewarded. Harmless as that sounds, it is the first step toward a theology of glory.

The theology of glory is a big thing on the religious scene today. But it sounds better than it is. The theology of glory suggests that if you are really a Christian (and you ought to be able to dig up some kind of "proof" that you are), then things are almost certain to go better for you in nearly every area of your life. You will go from one success to another, because God will pamper you, providing one goody after another, rewarding you for being a disciple. That's the way it will be, in our individual lives and for the church in this world. In other words, it pays to be a Christian.

But what happens when things don't work out that way? When the pay-off doesn't come? What happens when health or wealth or success elude our reach? What happens when, in fact, things go the other way, giving us pain and trouble and weakness? What a terrible turn our faith-life can take. How can you then square misfortune and suffering with being a Christian?

You can believe that the first century Christians were confronted with that perplexing problem. Instead of living vital, sun-tanned lives brimming over with prosperity, they experienced persecution. Persecution! Not only did that mean hardship and suffering, but it surprised the daylights out of them! They thought God should treat them better than that.

We still do. After we've committed our life to God in Christ, witnessed to our faith, we think that ought to be worth something but then life suddenly takes a turn for the worse, and we begin to wonder about this whole business. Obviously something's not right. Maybe we've attached ourselves to the wrong religion. Boarded the wrong plane! Maybe none of it is true. It sure doesn't look like it, not the way things are going.

Often when something goes wrong, we say, "This just isn't my day." The assumption seems to be that everything ought to go our way, and if it doesn't we feel victimized. When life doesn't seem to be working out the way we want it to, when we are foiled and frustrated and don't get the recognition we think we deserve, or when illness or hardship comes, then we start saying things like "maybe we don't understand what the Bible means by faith." Maybe we're not doing what we're supposed to be doing. Maybe our church hasn't taught us the right stuff, or maybe we don't believe enough, or aren't sincere enough. Perhaps we're not good enough. Maybe all that biblical propaganda about Jesus Christ isn't true! And so we are tempted to dump the whole business.

Isn't it supposed to pay to be religious, to be a Christian? Let's go to our gospel for this morning and take a new look at it.

The setting is the upper room just prior to Jesus' arrest in the Garden of Gethsemane. Judas has just left to make preparations for his betrayal of Christ. Our Lord then turns to the disciples and says, "Now the Son of Man's glory is revealed; now God's glory is revealed through him and he will do it at once," and from there he goes out to be arrested like a common felon, to be publicly flogged and ridiculed, and finally to be subjected to utter humiliation, as they hang him stark naked on a cross. Some glory! Some glory.

Now that's more than enough to blow our minds because to our way of thinking, what Jesus experienced is about as far from glory as you can get. In fact, the whole thing begins to sound pretty scary. Scary, because according to the Bible, our way of being in the world is supposed to be like Christ's. We, too, are to serve under the sign of the cross.

I recall a farmboy telling of the time he came out of his house and heard a commotion by the chicken coop. He ran quickly and found a hen being savagely attacked by a large hawk. He stopped, picked up a stick, and ran to the hen's defense, but he was too late; as the hawk flew off, the hen collapsed. The boy looked sadly at the stricken hen wondering to himself, wondering why the hen had not fled to the safety of the chicken coop which was only a few feet away. He knew why, when from under the wings of the dead hen emerged four little chicks and on each was a mark of blood, the blood of mother-love that sacrificed itself for their salvation.

We, too, are a marked people, marked by the blood of the Lamb of God who was crucified for us and gave himself in suffering love that we might be saved. We were marked in baptism as the pastor made the sign of the cross upon our forehead saying, "Receive the sign of the holy cross, that from this time onward, you shall know the Lord, the power of his resurrection, and the fellowship of his sufferings." So we are sealed by the Spirit and marked with the Cross of Christ forever. Well, what do you think the cross is a sign of? The cross is the sign of suffering love. That is the power we wield, we Christians who are Christ's body in this world, the power of suffering love!

There are easier routes to travel in our world. The easiest way is just to hang on, to hang on to what is ours, to hang on to privilege, to hang on to life, and to protect ourselves: from involvement, from caring, from suffering, from crosses. It's not hard to understand why so many are tempted to buy in to the theology of glory these days because it's the same old success story; if you are good, God will bless you with health and wealth, the whole ball of wax. But we are the baptized. We are marked by the glory of the cross. There we received our identity. There we were called to be God's children in this world, as Jesus was.

Of course if God bowed to our whims and rewarded the religious in terms of the depth of their faith, it would make it much easier to stand in judgment of one another. We could preach to the sick, like Job's friends, that if only they would repent of their sins, they would be made well. We could pounce on the poor with self-righteous indignation and inform them that success follows on the heels commitment to Jesus Christ; the better you are, the better God likes you, and the more you are given.

What a hideous heresy! Imagine, reducing God's steadfast love to fickle favor, a favor which the Lord trickles into our lives in proportion to our faithfulness and/or how well we are behaving ourselves. Given the difficult and impoverished lives of the early Christians, it soon became clear to them that the world's idea of glory stood in stark contrast to the glory of the cross. As Paul discovered, "The message of the cross is foolishness to those who are perishing, but to us who are being saved it is the power of God. Consider your call, not many of you were wise, not many were powerful, not many were of noble birth. But God chose what is foolish in the world to shame the wise; God chose what is weak in the world to shame the strong; God chose what is low and despised in the world, things that are not, to reduce to nothing things that are (1 Corinthians 1:18, 26-28).''

Clearly the glory to which we are called is a strange kind of glory, rooted not in our goodness but in God's faithfulness, and characterized not by success but by servanthood, not by golden health but by ready helpfulness. The desire for the things that mark privilege and success in this world and the quest for health are all dangerous temptations that threaten our ability to see the kind of life God in Christ has in mind for us.

This concept is illustrated cleverly in the story of Horville Sash. Horville had a very humble job in the offices of the largest corporation of the world. He worked as the go-fer in the lowest reaches of the building doing what he could to help other people do their jobs, but often he wondered and thought about the floor just above his.

Then came a day when Horville found a bug scurrying across the floor. As the mail room clerk, Horville had only bugs to command — to bully. He raised his foot to flatten the helpless speck. "Spare me." The bug spoke. A speaking bug? Horville spared the bug. His reward: a wish. "I wish to be promoted to the second floor." Granted. Horville's boss told him that very day. Horville marched to the second floor like MacArthur and Patton rolled into one.

Wait. Horville heard footsteps on the ceiling of floor number two. There was a third floor. A higher level meant higher wages, more power. The next day, Horville rose to the third floor job of sales coordinator. But he wasn't satisfied, he now knew there were other floors, many others and the promotions were like kerosene to a flame. He went to the 10th floor, then to the 20th, the 50th, the 70th. Horville sat by the indoor pool on floor 96. The next day Horville discovered, and it was only by chance, a stairway leading up — to another floor? He scrambled up the stairs. He was on the roof. He was now the highest, the most powerful. Content. Horville headed for the stairway. Just as he turned to go back down to his office he saw a boy near the edge of the building with his eyes closed. "What are you doing?" "Praying." "To whom?" The boy answered, pointing a finger skyward, "To God."

Panic gripped Horville. Was there a floor above him? He couldn't see it. Just clouds. He couldn't hear the shuffling of feet. "Do you mean there's an authority above me?" "Yes." The bug was summoned, "Make me God. Make me the highest," he said. "Put me in the type of position that only God would hold if he were on earth."

The very next day, Horville began work as a go-fer in the basement![1]

The glory of God is that he came to love us and serve us. His work was as a go-fer in the basement of this world, as it were. For God came to identify with the lonely, the outcasts, the poor and the powerless. And it is our glory to live like him.

A father overheard his two sons playing church. One of them was explaining to the other what all the parts of the liturgy were about. "Do you know what it means at the end of the service when the pastor does this?" he asked, making the sign of the cross. "It means some of you go out this way, and some of you go out that way."

The lad was right. The cross sends us and scatters us out into the world. Someone has said that the really important thing for any church is not how many it seats but how many it sends, with a strange-looking power, the greatest power the world has known, the power of suffering love. So we are sent, you and I, sent to live out our Lord's kind of whimsical and yet lavish grace and with the glory of being marked with the cross, a strange-looking glory sought by few, but which is glory indeed. Amen.

---

1. Printed in *The Clergy Journal* from a sermon by C. Thomas Hilton.

Easter 6
John 14:23-29

A Farewell Gift

I have never liked saying "goodbye," it always elicits feelings of finality. So I say other things like, "See you!" or "Hope to see you sometime." Most of the time I like quick goodbyes. However, when a loved one leaves there are no formalities. We embrace, sometimes through tears. It is not uncommon to cast out cliches, often with a bit of humor, to lighten the atmosphere. But in the end the word "goodbye" is bound to be spoken.

It's a comforting thought really, because it is a shortened form of "God be with you." In fact the farewell in many languages express the same thing. "The Spanish, *adios* means 'to God' — meaning that our lives are in his keeping. And *vaya con dios* means 'go with God.' Benedictions at the close of our worship, are reminders that as we part from one another God goes with each one of us."[1]

Our gospel story this morning is also a time of parting. Jesus and the disciples are gathered in the upper room just prior to his betrayal, arrest and crucifixion. It will all happen quickly. The atmosphere is tense; the disciples know that something ominous is about to happen. They are troubled and at a loss for words. With characteristic compassion, Jesus lays aside his own intense feelings and reaches out to comfort his followers.

"I am leaving," says Jesus, "but you will not be alone. God will send the Advocate, the Holy Spirit, to teach you all things and will remind you of everything. I am also leaving you with something to remember me by — a farewell gift. It is precious beyond all measure. Don't be troubled. Don't be afraid. I am giving you the gift of peace." Jesus then goes on to say that the world doesn't really understand the kind of peace he is giving.

When we think of peace we usually think of the absence of war between nations, or the ending of hostilities between persons. Even though the Cold War continues, some politicians speak of our time as a period of peace. But we know better don't we?

Two youngsters get into a fight and the teacher runs out and says, "Now cut that out. I want you two to quit fighting, make up and shake hands." Under the threat of the teacher's punishment the two boys may indeed quit fighting. They may even shake hands and walk away in a peaceful manner. But beneath their tranquil exteriors the feelings which ignited the conflict may still be raging out of control. Inside they may be experiencing a whole host of emotions: dislike, fear, revenge and anger. The two boys part in "peace" but they do not experience it.

The peace of which Jesus speaks is not simply the end of conflict nor is it, for that matter, even the lack of inner struggle. The peace of God is an internal strength and tranquility which exists in spite of turmoil whether in the world around us or deep within us. An old story which illustrates this point concerns a little boy who sat calmly aboard a ship which was tossed about like a toothpick by the wind and waves. Another passenger asked him, "Aren't you worried? Doesn't the storm frighten you?"

"No," replied the boy. "If I sit here I can look through that hole and I can see the captain at the helm. He is my father, and he has brought this ship through many storms. As long as my father is at the helm he will get us safely through; I am not afraid."

We not only have trouble understanding what Jesus means by peace, we also have a tendency to view peace as a requirement of faith. In other words, instead of seeing peace as a gift, we see it as a command. If you are a Christian you will have peace!

I recall the story of a little girl who, when trains were popular transportation, was taking her first train ride with her parents. As night descended, the mother took the girl, who was clearly quite anxious, and placed her on the upper bunk of the sleeper. She told her little one that up there she would be nearer to God and that God would watch over her.

As silence enveloped the young lady she became afraid and called softly, "Mommy, are you there?"

"Yes dear," came the response.

A little later, in a louder voice, the child called, "Daddy, are you there, too?"

"Yes dear," was the reply.

After this had been repeated several times one of the passengers sharing their sleeper car finally lost his patience and shouted loudly, "Yes, we're all here, your father, your mother, your brother, and all your aunts and cousins; now settle down and go to sleep!"

There was a moment of silence and then, in hushed tones a little voice asked, "Mommy, was that God?"

Jesus, in offering peace, does not say, "I'm here, the Holy Spirit's here and God is here, now be at peace!" The peace that Jesus offers cannot be had simply by desiring. The peace of God is a gift, it can only be received as a by-product of faith. That's why the world is largely a stranger to it.

Most of the world sees peace as an end in itself, a release from tension, the avoidance of struggle, an escape from pain: the peace of contentment. So we are bombarded with all kinds of promises for peace in the forms of aspirins, laxatives, drugs, legal and illegal, all kinds of diversions. We have been so pampered that at the slightest pain, or provocation or indication of boredom we are urged to pop a pill, take a drink, buy this or that to overcome our discomfort. So we search our world with its glamorous promises for some ease, some respite — the peace of contentment.

Now what is so bad about that? What is wrong with wanting to feel good? Life is hard, why not try to avoid its struggle? Why shouldn't we try to combat its boredom? Why not alleviate its pains?

A seminary professor once said, "You Americans are so spoiled. You think that suffering is bad. That is not always true. Suffering is never comfortable but in this world it is unavoidable, and sometimes, if you face it rightly, it can even be beneficial. Nietzsche was playing with truth when he said, 'What ever does not kill us makes us stronger.' Suffering becomes destructive when it drives a person into one's self isolating them from God and those they love. But suffering can also be positive if faith and love create the power to overcome it. The heroes and heroines of history are not those who took it easy, who had it good, but those who struggled and who overcame seemingly insurmountable odds."

A striking example is the Russian novelist Fyodor Dostoyevsky regarded by many as one of the greatest literary genuises of all time. His books are classics. *The Brothers Karamazov* is regarded by many as the greatest novel ever written. His stories all have a similar theme, that our redemption is to be found through suffering, not simply physical suffering, but in the anguish of our selfhood. We become fully human, Dostoyevsky believed, by being tested and being strengthened through it.[2]

The peace which Jesus gave to the disciples involved very little contentment. They had to endure persecutions, misunderstanding and hardships of every kind. Perhaps that is why Jesus says, "Come unto me all you who are weary and burdened and I will give you rest." Notice he didn't say, "Come unto me all you who are contented, who have been able to avoid the tensions and struggles of life." He tells us to come if we are life-weary and he will give us rest. The Greek word translated "rest" points to being refreshed and revitalized rather than finding relaxation. He tells us that we may come to him for strength if we bear heavy burdens. His promise is regeneration for those at the end of their tether, and peace for those who struggle.

Perhaps the best illustration comes from Paul's own life. This scrawny little man with a whole host of ailments, troubled by his "thorn in the flesh," and constantly beleaguered by those who were out to destroy him, once cried out, "O wretched man that I am who will deliver me from this body of death (Romans 7:24)!" Later he would write, "I have learned in whatever state I am to be content, I have learned the secret of facing hunger and want (Philippians 4:12)." And again, "I have fought the good fight, I have finished the race, I have kept the faith. From now on there is reserved for me the crown of righteousness (2 Timothy 4:7-8)."

Paul experienced serenity of soul not because he took the easy way out, but because he met head on the tribulations and tensions of the world, and by the power of God, overcame them. Paul said the peace he experienced was "beyond human understanding" because it was not simply the absence of hostilities and distress, it was not produced within himself, but was an amazing gift given by Christ through faith.

I remind you of that good news today: for the promise still stands. Our Lord says today, as he did long ago, "My peace I give to you . . ." But as we hear those words of invitation I remind you that the way to peace is not the way of comfort and contentment. The gospel meets us with high demands for service and sacrifice. We start at the Cross, and we must never forget that. This symbol of our faith is a sign of defeat, and a reminder of the most tragic event in history. Yet this is where our peace begins, because it was there, on the cross, in the ultimate tension, in the monumental struggle between God and Satan that Jesus became victorious and opened the doorway to life eternal.

It is the resurrected, living Lord who beckons us offering rejuvenation for our haggard spirits, and strength to cope with the difficulties of our lives. He does not offer us a rocking chair and a cup of tea, with sweet music in the background. Just the opposite! He says, "Follow me!" And this is true for everyone. It does no good to say, "I've done my share, I've borne my burdens . . . now is time to rest." As long as you have life, you have an active role to fulfill in God's eternal plan. You must not pull the draperies around your soul and passively sit down with it. Jesus calls us to love our neighbors, those in need, and tells us that we have been commissioned to carry out a mission of mercy in his name. You see, God's farewell gift was definitely not intended to promote the life of relaxation, or ease, or of peace as the world offers it.

But Christ accompanies us into the conflict. He speaks of sin, and then forgives us. He speaks of love, and then gives us the ministry of reconciliation. He speaks of weakness, and then calls us to share the burdens of those around us, bringing his power to our inadequacies. He recruits us to do battle against the evils of this world, but he promises strength, and a peace which is beyond our understanding. It is in active service, where we put our faith on the line, that we discover that in all things we are held by God, that always underneath, "underneath are the everlasting arms (Deuteronomy 33:27)."

I read some time ago of a recording that is used in maternity hospitals to stop mass crying in the nursery. When one infant after another begins to howl in a growing din, this recording is played. Within moments they are all quiet. What is the music, the theme that is played? It is a recording of a mother's heartbeat as heard by the fetus within the womb before it was born. Apparently the infant's cry of terror in a new environment is stilled by the sense of security evoked by the sound of a mother's heartbeat.

So it is with the Christian. Amid the struggles, great and small, which we face every day, we need to stop our frantic activity and take time to let our Lord embrace us through the Holy Spirit. Through faith we feel the heartbeat of God's love and rest secure, knowing that all things belong to God. Then a wonderful thing happens. As we surrender our burdens to God, they are replaced with a gift, the farewell gift that Jesus left with his disciples. While it is a gift with ancient origins it has a power which continually regenerates it so that it is brand new for you and me. Even more, it's a gift that keeps on giving. It is the gift of peace, a peace which the world cannot give or understand, but as Jesus said, neither could the world take it away.

The peace of Christ which passes all understanding, keeps your hearts and your minds in Christ Jesus. Amen.

1. *Pulpit Resource,* Vol. 12, No. 2, p. 41. Logos Art Productions, Inver Grove, Minnesota.

2. *Pulpit Resource,* Vol. 9, No. 2, pp. 14-15. Logos Art Productions, Inver Grove, Minnesota.

Easter 7
John 17:20-26

Beyond Togetherness

There's a story which many of you have heard and it is a fitting introduction for our text. A group of new arrivals in heaven met Saint Peter at the Pearly Gates. He began to show them around, pointing out areas of interest and filling them in on the rules of the kingdom. There were many "oohs" and "aahs" from the crowd, and they were obviously enjoying themselves immensely. Suddenly Saint Peter stopped a short distance from a massive building which was miles wide, long and high, and without doors or windows. "While we pass this building," he said, "you must walk quietly and utter not so much as a sound." So the entourage tiptoed obediently past the monolith without a word.

Once they were past, however, an inquisitive soul inquired, "Why did we have to be so quiet when we passed that building?"

Saint Peter responded, "God put the (name a denomination here) in there; they think they're the only ones up here."

It isn't just (name a denomination here) who think they are the only ones who have got this God business right. There are other denominations who also give the impression of exclusiveness and project the feeling that it is only natural that the blessings of God should fall upon them. They are probably just as amazed as we are to see that it "rains on the just and the unjust alike (Matthew 5:45)."

I suppose that is not strange, since we have been brought up on a diet of theological ingredients which are not only palatable for us but have come highly recommended by God; at least that's what our clergy tell us. So we are suspect of those who indulge in denominational dishes of a different sort.

It is important to realize, however, that God's docrtinal tastes are not so narrow. According to Jesus, all who love the name of the Lord are welcomed. Notice, that while he wants us all to be one with him and the Father, he doesn't suggest that our unity is dependent upon our ability to develop a theological recipe which all Christians everywhere could find tasty enough so that we all can feast together as one, a gigantic universal church.

In other words our unity need not be the result of sitting down at the negotiating table and trying to map out a theological menu for the church that would appeal to all concerned. Bishop William Temple, Archbishop of Canterbury, once said, "We meet in committees and construct our schemes of union; in face of the hideous fact of Christian divisions we are driven to this; but how paltry are our efforts compared with the call of God! The way to the union of Christendom does not lie through committee rooms, although there are tasks to be done there, it lies through personal union with the Lord so deep and real as to be comparable with his union with the Father . . . ."[1]

Temple has penetrated through the superficial. His sense of union in Christ is beyond togetherness. He moves past even the appealing call to our common humanity, illustrated most commonly in the words of Pastor John Donne many years ago, ". . . No person is an Island entire of himself; every one is a piece of the Continent, a part of the main. If a clump of dirt be washed away by the Sea, Europe is the Less, as well as if a Mountain were, as well as if a House of your friends or your own were; any person's death diminishes me, because I am involved in Humankind; and therefore never send for whom the bell tolls; It tolls for thee."[2]

The unity for which Jesus prays is deeper, richer and more consuming than "sharing the same skin" a la Donne and it certainly is not dependent upon a huge organizational world church infrastructure. Rather Jesus' desire for a union of people is founded upon the Word of God with faith as the way in which we come to understand that we have been brought into close relationship with God and the world.

The point is, more than merely sharing a common humanity, God in Christ has brought us together into the intimate unity of the family of God. Our adoption as children of God, and therefore as members of the royal household, was accomplished when "God sent forth his Son, born of woman (Galatians 4:5)." Baptism becomes the unifying act which places us all into the same family, makes us all blood relatives who have been bonded together by the shedding of Christ's blood on Calvary. This is no mere genetic affiliation, this is a dynamic creation, constituted by Christ, which shall last for ever and ever.

The genius of God's plan is obvious. If we recognize that we are all members of the same family, if we acknowledge that God desires to hold us in a single peace then, ideally, we will stop fighting with each other and destroying one another and instead begin standing with one another and working together to bring people to Christ and to become an answer to prayer for those who cry out to God for help.

However, if your family is like my family, your day-to-day operation is not marked with constant good will and cooperation. Parents can disagree with each other, or the children, or the youngsters with each other. There are so many possibilities for dissension — goals will vary, opinions often differ and wills may clash. I think the reason for the popularity of the television cartoon "The Simpsons" is that it lays bare some of the battles which are fought in the arenas of many homes. Apparently there is some comfort in knowing that others experience problems similar to one's own. But if love is at the heart of our relationships, and forgiveness is liberally applied, there is still a family unity and loyalty which acts like a glue — unity holds family members together even when they are apart and loyalty brings them together again at times of crisis or joyful celebration.

The church as the family of God has characteristics similar to other family units but with infinitely more possibilities for disagreement and dissension. It is no wonder then that Paul saw the primary task of the church as one of reconciliation: "All this is from God, who through Christ reconciled us to himself and gave us the ministry of reconciliation. So we are ambassadors for Christ, God making his appeal through us (2 Corinthians 5:18-20)."

To reconcile is to bring into harmony, not into unison, two opposing parties or points of view. There is a difference between the two concepts. "Reconciliation is not making everyone 'sing' in unison. It is to enable everyone to 'sing' in harmony. Reconciliation doesn't erase differences; it seeks to bring them into workable accord. The world will always have opposites. You will never get opposites to 'sing' in unison, nor would you necessarily want to. To do so might be to destroy individual contributions and needed correctives. But polarities can be brought into harmony — where differences, strengths, uniqueness, and distinctions can be blended into melodic composition."[3]

God has given us the responsibility of declaring the good news that because Jesus died for us all, we have already been reconciled, brought into harmony with God. And because of that we are further given the goal of being reconciled to one another. That is the unity for which Jesus prays. The world's inhabitants need to recognize that we are all one family in God, regardless of color, or denomination or worship preferences. We may not always sing the same musical line, but we are to seek harmony until we become a universe, a uni-verse, one verse, one song in praise of God's awesome grace in Jesus Christ.

So our calling begins with reconciliation, calling people home to share God's love, joining with other Christian churches in declaring the glory of Christ till all are moved to join with us in living out the goodness of God. But part of our oneness in Christ also includes unity of purpose. Friedrich Nietzsche once said, in effect, "It would be easier to believe in your Redeemer if you looked more redeemed." On the other foot that means it will be easier for others to believe in the Savior when you bear not only his creative word, but also his loving presence into the world.

One man suggested that the ecumenical movement was a sideshow with theologians sitting around splitting doctrinal hairs when they should be planning strategies for ministering to the needs of the poor for food, shelter, compassion, companionship and understanding. "In this shared vision of response to the needs of others," he said, "we become one indeed."

That is the glory of which Jesus said, "The glory which thou has given me I have given to them," the glory of being the incarnate presence of God, the answer to prayer for the millions who cry out to God for mercy every hour. That is not glory as the world usually speaks of it but it is glory indeed for the needs of the world are monumental and those who sacrifice to minister to the needy are most like Christ.

There is, however, the other side of the equation. While we are to be, as Luther said, "little Christs" to the world, we are also, according to Jesus to see Christ in "the least of these who are members of my family (Matthew 25:31ff)." We need to have one word of caution. So often we think of the poor, the needy, the dispossessed as persons "out there." If we look around us we will see that there are also many persons who need us "in here." I'm reminded of the story J. D. Salinger tells in *Franny and Zooey.*

Franny and Zooey are members of the Glass family which had been featured on the radio show, "It's a Wise Kid." Years later Franny suffers an emotional collapse and Zooey, trying to bring her out of it, reminds her of those days. He brings to mind how Seymour told him how to shine their shoes for the Fat Lady in the radio audience, a person they did not know but who felt she knew them because of the program. "He never did tell me who the Fat Lady was, but I shined my shoes for the Fat Lady every time I went on the air again . . . . This terribly clear, clear picture of the Fat Lady formed in my mind . . . and she probably had cancer. Anyway, it seemed clear why Seymour wanted me to shine my shoes when I went on the air. It made sense."

The memory stirs something in Franny; she remembers how her Fat Lady had cancer, too. "But," says Zooey, "I'll tell you a terrible secret — are you listening to me? There isn't anyone out there who isn't Seymour's Fat Lady. There isn't anyone anywhere that isn't Seymour's Fat Lady. Don't you know that? Don't you know that secret yet? And don't you know — *listen* to me, now — *don't you know who that Fat Lady really is?* It's Christ himself. Christ himself."[4]

So we are committed to reach out to everyone everywhere; all are included in the encompassing love of God, those who agree with us and those who don't. We reach out with God's Word to those whose lifestyles comform with ours as well as those that don't. Our response to Jesus is to proclaim the good news of the sacrificial love of God to the down-and-out as well as the up-and-in. We are to minister to the needs of all members of this congregation but our concern is to spill over into the community and into other lands because God's love knows no boundaries, denominational or otherwise.

The prayer of Christ for unity does not compel us to rush to the negotiating table in an attempt to reduce our Christian differences to a bland recipe of faith which offends no one so that we end up with a church that is weak and powerless. The oneness for which Jesus so yearns is something beyond togetherness. In fact unity is not even something we can decide to do or work toward. Being made one with Christ is something that has already been accomplished; it is up to us to accept it and begin to live it! Therefore we are called forward to proclaim the good news that God has reconciled the world to himself and in harmony work with one another in carrying out Christ's merciful ministry to the world. In the words of Emmett Jarrett, "Our unity is God's gift, because it reflects the unity of Jesus with the Father, without which we are nothing. Let us pray for that unity, of suffering and glory, of faith and of service, in love and in hope."[5]

---

1. Quoted from a sermon by the Rev. Emmet Jarret in *Selected Sermons*, May 11, 1986. Parish Supplies, New York.

2. An adaptation from *Major British Writers*, Harcourt, Brace and Company, 1959. p. 392.

3. *Pulpit Resource*, Vol. 11, No. 1, Inver Hills, Minnesota. p. 37.

4. Sallinger, J.D. *Franny and Zooey*. Little, Brown and Co., Boston, Massachusetts. 1961. pp. 198-200.

5. Jarrett, Emmett, *Selected Sermons, May 11, 1986, Parish Supplies, New York.*

Pentecost
John 14:8-17, 25-27 [C]
John 15:26-27; 16:4b-11 [L]
John 20:19-23 [RC]

The Greatest Wonder Of All!

The celebration of Pentecost, with its mighty demonstration of power by the Holy Spirit, is a good time to reflect on some of the mighty deeds of God, because God's awe-inspiring acts aren't all locked back there in the memory banks of Bible history buffs; they are still happening all around us. Discovering them is a real adventure because we all, young and old, tend to be impressed by that which is uncommon, unusual or extraordinary. I recall seeing a youngster holding a popcorn kernel in his fingers; he was looking at it with admiration. "What's up?" I asked. "It's hard to believe," he said, "that a fluffy piece of popcorn is in this hard kernel."

This is a wonder, but it typifies how our myopia causes us to be mystified by minor marvels, when the profound mysteries of God are left unexplored and unappreciated. God is the master of mystery and specializes in making the usual, unusual, the common, uncommon and the ordinary, extraordinary.

Have you ever thought about the mind-boggling things which God has been able to do, and with such incredible ease? I'm speaking here of unbelievable things as when God uttered a word and a universe exploded into being, a universe so vast that scientists describe it in terms of infinity, space without end. The Bible says that when that happened, "the morning stars sang together and all the heavenly beings shouted for joy (Job 38:7)."

Or consider when God entered the world as a little baby. Every birth is indeed miraculous but when the Christ-child was born the concept of time was shattered, literally split in two. From Christ's birth onward we have measured time as B.C.

(before Christ) and A.D. (in the year of our Lord). And you will remember that at that incredible moment legions of angels sang a victory song to an uncomprehending world.

Time after astounding time the Bible illustrates how God, with singular deftness, delved into the arena of human activity and brought about momumental changes which left the people awestruck and gasping for breath. The Day of Pentecost was one of those times. Let us consider the texts for this most amazing day and look anew at the truths they express to see how God has included you and me in the greatest wonder of all.

We begin in the Old Testament with the story of the Tower of Babel (Genesis 11:1-9). We are told the nations of the world were given the gift of a common language which they unfortunately used to "make a name for themselves" and thus declare their independence from God. In loving kindness the Lord God prevented their treason simply by touching their tongues and causing such confusion that they "scattered abroad over the face of all the earth (v. 9)." Notice what child's play it was for the Spirit of God to mingle with the syllables of human language and change the course of history forever!

Thousands of years later God worked a remarkable reversal of that miracle. On the day which we now call the Day of Pentecost (Acts 2:1-11), the Holy Spirit came in the rush of a mighty wind and created what looked like tongues of fire which "rested" on each one of the disciples. When they began to speak the Spirit manipulated their words so that their message was understood by people from all over the known world. The Bible says that they "were bewildered because each one heard (the apostles) speaking in (his or her) own language (v. 6)." The seeds of salvation had been sown among the nations; now the divided could be united, the alienated could be reconciled, the self-centered could become other-centered. It was just what the apostles needed to jar them out of their ethnic, parochial concept of what God had commissioned them to do. It became unmistakably clear that their mission field was nothing less than the world. And God brought about that history-making event with characteristic ease, but in such a giddy way, that the disciples were thought to be drunk!

However, greater wonders await us! On the Day of Pentecost, the Holy Spirit only set the stage. The initial thrust of the gospel into the world had been accomplished, but that was only the beginning. What of the nations unaware, and the millions as yet unborn? The entire world had been liberated from the immobilizing power of sin and the haunting specter of death through the resurrection of our Lord Jesus Christ, but how could all its inhabitants become aware of this glorious victory?

During World War II a large number of Japanese soldiers sequestered themselves in caves on the Philippine Islands, cut off from chains of command and supply routes. They were on their own, and were committed to the defense of those islands at the cost of their lives if need be. When the war was over, the problem became how to notify and convince those soldiers that the hostilities had ended. The atomic scientist J. Robert Oppenheimer once observed, "The best way to send an idea is to wrap it up in a person." That is what they did. The news was spread by the Japanese, cave by cave, person by person.

Jesus understood this dynamic; he was God's message of love wrapped up in a person. So before he left our planet, he gathered his disciples and made an amazing announcement. The incredible news? God will send the Holy Spirit to engage human hearts and minds and tongues empowering them to witness of the mighty deeds of God in loving and saving the world. "You also are witnesses," says Jesus (John 15:27). "As the Father sent me, even so send I you (John 20:21)." "Those who believe in me will also do the works that I do; and greater works than these will he do (John 14:12)."

We, too, have been given the privilege, responsibility and dignity of being vessels in which God chooses to dwell. How's that for a mind-blowing concept? Through the power of the Holy Spirit, we are invited to take part in the mighty enterprise of bringing the message of salvation to the world. We are not given secondary roles, we are placed on the front line in the diplomatic corps of our Lord! Paul explained it this way, "We are ambassadors for Christ, God making his appeal through us (2 Corinthians 5:20).'' Our Lord promises that the dynamic power of the Holy Spirit will use our witness, meager as it may sometimes be, so that we become agents of God's good news to a world which is continually cowed by bad news.

So the first thing we must keep in mind is that the Holy Spirit is truly transfiguring. You and I are able to offer our witness to others without having to be concerned about saying the "right" words or doing the "right" things, as long as we are sharing the goodness and mercy of God. The Spirit can take even simple offerings and transform them into experiences which can shape and color and warm the lives of others. Let me illustrate.

Douglas Maurer, 15, of Creve Coeur, Missouri, had been feeling bad for several days. Mrs. Maurer took Douglas to the hospital in St. Louis where he was diagnosed as having leukemia.

The doctors told him in frank terms about his disease. They said that for the next three years, he would have to undergo chemotherapy. They didn't sugercoat the side effects. They told Douglas he would go bald and that his body would most likely bloat. Upon learning this, he went into a deep depression.

His aunt called a floral shop to send Douglas an arrangement of flowers. She told the clerk that it was for her teenage nephew who had leukemia. When the flowers arrived at the hospital, they were beautiful. Douglas read the card from his aunt without emotion. Then he noticed a second card. It said: "Douglas — I took your order. I work at Brix Florist. I had leukemia when I was seven years old. I'm 22 years old now. Good Luck. My heart goes out to you. Sincerely, Laura Bradley."

His face lit up. "Oh wow!" he said.

It's interesting: Douglas Maurer was in a hospital filled with millions of dollars of the most sophisticated technological equipment. He was being treated by expert doctors and nurses with competent medical training. But it was a sales clerk in a flower shop, a young woman making $170 a week, who — by taking the time to care, and by being willing to go with what her heart told her to do — gave Douglas hope and the will to carry on.[1]

Wonderful and heart-warming as that story is, the disciples were commissioned to do more than lift up people's spirits. Their mission was a message, a message which needed to be spoken and written in every tongue so that all people might hear the gospel, the good news of how God saved us through Jesus Christ, in their own language. In other words the world was to be their congregation!

The content of the apostle's message, says Jesus was to "convince the world of sin, and of righteousness and judgment (John 16:8)." That may sound confusing because we tend to think of sin and judgment in negative ways. However, a word of judgment can awaken a sinner to their need for God and then it becomes good news because they discover that, in God's righteousness, they have been liberated from all the bondages of this world forever.

So off the disciples went with God's message to fulfill a task that must have seemed insurmountable. It would have been easy for them to have given up before they started. But Jesus stated clearly that they were to begin where they were: "But you shall receive power when the Holy Spirit has come upon you; and you shall be my witnesses in Jerusalem and in all Judea and Samaria and to the end of the earth (Acts 1:8)." Our Lord helped them to get a perspective on their mission: begin in your own backyard.

Thus the second thing we hang on to as we accept the commission of Christ is that we don't start out by taking on the whole world. We keep that goal always before us, but we start right here, among our own members, in our own homes, in our own community. Even that may seem too difficult a task, too large and too threatening. Let me assure you, with the Spirit's blessing we can do far more than we imagine. So in carrying out our mission it is important that we do not let the enormity of the task keep us from doing something.

I like the story reported in a documentary film on the Nobel Peace Prize winner, Mother Teresa. A young man who had gone to India to help her in her mission to the poor and sick was interviewed. He had been given the task of working with a small group of eight or 10 boys who were homeless and parentless. He became a parent, teacher, minister and friend to them — living with them, bringing them up. When a reporter asked the young man if there were not times when he felt discouraged as he realized how many thousands of children there were whom he could not help, a look came over the young man's face which seemed to say, "That is about the most stupid question I have ever heard." What he finally did say echoed the words of Mother Teresa, "Here are some boys who need me. I am able to help them. That is all that matters."

As Christians we begin by witnessing to Christ where we work, where we play, where we worship, but we also band together in congregations to enlarge our ministry. You can only do so much but with your tithes or offerings the church can send others to go where you cannot. Remember, Jesus says his message is to the whole world. The Spirit is always seeking new apostles, so I caution you, young and old, keep your ears open. You never know when God, in a still small voice, might call you to some high and noble task somewhere else in the world.

The apostles certainly began their mission with fear and trembling. The political forces which had brought about the death of Jesus were still in power. The Hebrew religous institution was still antagonistic and had pledged to wipe out the Jesus sect.

The signs of terrible struggle were all around them. But their resolve to carry out Christ's command to evangelize the world was bolstered by the fact that, for 40 days after the resurrection, he had mysteriously glided in and out of their lives, giving them the security of knowing that he was with them and would never be far from them at any time.

I have heard from many persons who say that one of the most difficult places to witness is at home. So the third thing we need to remember is that our Lord is with us as powerfully as he was with the first disciples. We are not asked to do more than we can but whatever we offer to God will be blessed, often in ways beyond our understanding. We don't need fancy words, just a willing heart. We don't need a lot of theology, we need to let those who share our home know we care about them for Jesus' sake. A loving spirit can do more for the kingdom of God than barbed preaching.

For those of you old enough to remember, think back with me to the end of World War II. What if you had been chosen to spread the news, "The war is over; a truce has been declared!" That would have been so exciting you would hardly have been able to contain yourself. You would have run out gladly, jubilantly with the message. So you are sent by Christ, not to preach to others, but to simply declare that the "war" is over and share with them the joy of what God has done for you.

Some years ago I was searching for a member of the church council; a certain matter needed immediate attention. I was told he was in a particular bar. I could see and feel the embarrassment of the patrons as I walked in, but it needed to be done. After a brief consultation with the man I turned to walk out. As I reached the door, the barmaid called out, "Can I talk to you?"

"Sure," I responded and walked over to the lady who I had never seen before. She looked me square in the eye and spoke rapidly, "I'm Agness Backlo, I know you're a pastor. I don't belong to any church but my husband Obed used to be a member of your denomination. He has cancer and I was wondering if you would be willing to go to see him at our house?" I agreed to do so as long as he was told that I was coming.

My relationship with Agnes and Obed deepened as his cancer worsened. Once a week I would call. Then one evening I answered the telephone and heard a distraught voice say, "I'm calling from the VA hospital, Obed is much worse. The doctor says he is going to die tonight." Without hesitation I responded, "I'll be there as fast as I can."

It took better than an hour to cover the distance between my home and the VA hospital, but when I arrived he was still conscious. We had communion together while Agnes looked on, tears pouring down her cheeks. Within the hour Obed died.

Three weeks after the funeral I made a call on Agnes. She said, in her typical staccato way, "I want to be baptized. We weren't even members and you cared for us, and your members gave us a fine funeral. They were so nice even though I didn't belong. I want to find out what makes people do that kind of thing. I want to join your church."

After eight weeks a beaming Agnes became a member of the church. Shortly thereafter I began receiving telephone calls. They all had the same basic pattern, "Pastor, this is Agnes. There's a family that needs help, could you go out and talk to them?" In every case one member of the family had been in a local bar and heard Agnes tell them of the joy she now experienced as a Christian. I kept track of the calls. In two years she sent me all over the countryside to 23 families. As a result of those visits, many people were baptized or confirmed and received into membership. Who knows how many people she has led to Christ in the years since?

We tend to be impressed by the colossal and phenomenal, the earth-shaking, but what greater wonder can there be that an uneducated barmaid who found her peace in Jesus and led over two dozen others to her Lord. That is a minor miracle!

We ought not, however, be surprised. God's promises come true. And as we witness, you and I in our everyday ways, the Spirit transforms these nouns, adjectives and verbs and does the mighty works of God. That, my dear friends, is the greatest wonder of all, that we are the bearers of life-transforming news which can change the destiny of people forever! As for our part, we should be honored and humbled that God should deem us worthy and use our witness as a means of bearing Christ's beauty and love to the world. Amen.

---

1. Bob Greene, "From Sufferer to Another," *Chicago Tribune,* August 1987 as printed in *Pulpit Resource,* Vol. 18, No. 2, Logos Productions, Inver Grove Heights, Minnesota. p. 31.